Ins and outs of Institutional Investing

Dean LeBaron

Ins and outs of Institutional Investing

Nelson
Hall
Chicago

LIBRARY OF CONGRESS CATALOGING IN PUBLICATION DATA

LeBaron, Dean.
    Ins and outs of institutional investing.

    Includes index.
    1.   Institutional investments—United States.
I.   Title.
HG4910.L43   332.6′327   76-40961
ISBN 0-88229-343-5

Manufactured in the United States of America

To Francis and Blake . . .
my bridges to the past and the future.

Contents

Acknowledgments

Key influences, without whom this work would not have been started nor finished, are Charles D. Ellis, President of Greenwich Research Associates who has goaded me into a number of activities, usually by superior example, and Peter Wyckoff of Bridgewater, Vermont, who provided the early motivation and editorial help, and without whom I might have walked away from the typewriter in the first few days. Any sparkle in the anecodotes will be more familiar to readers of Peter's works than of my own.

My wife, Emily, and children, Blake and Stacy, were very supportive.

Thanks go to all those investment colleagues mentioned and unmentioned who participated in the events and learning discussed in the book, particularly my associates at Batterymarch Financial Management whose investment activity allowed the leisure required to write it. I thank also Lynne Johnson for her assistance.

I have necessarily relied upon memory which may be conveniently selective. In order to create readable scenes, I have relied upon poetic license to recreate the tone and substance of conversations.

Introduction

Institutional investing involves changing events, big dollars, and wits sharpened by high stakes. Institutions dominate the current scene and they seem sinister and mysterious to the outsider. Often enough, they even confuse the insiders.

This book is intended as a real-life account of how institutional investors operate—particularly during the present period of dramatic change as institutional investors feel threatened by external forces affecting their lives and work.

The academic has continually considered himself to be the sole underpaid advocate of the rationality of security markets. The investment practitioner, essentially institutional in nature, has considered the academic as a challenger. Lately, the split has been contracting: academics and practitioners are drifting together. I recently spent a day at a university seminar on "efficient markets" where there were perhaps twenty-five participants, half academic and half practitioner. Small though these numbers were, such a meeting would not have taken place five years ago.

The split was caused, in part, by the fantasy that investment practitioners are omniscient. They believe, with some merit, that if the alchemy they perform to turn pencil lead into gold or conventional wisdom into profit were understood, they would all be unemployed. Investment managers have surrounded themselves with elaborate and expensive ceremonials which, although related to good results in the past, seem to have lost their potency. Just as the drought questions the value of the priest's rain dance, so does a bear market humble the professional investor.

The climate is perfect for a balanced review of how institutional investing really operates. I assume that, just as those who ride in commercial planes want to know what happens in the cockpit, so do all students and investors want to increase their awareness of what happens on the investment flight deck. Only if we can examine the real process can we hope to make improvements.

1

The Corporate
Environment

Wall Street is a topsy-turvy place where that which
seems right to do is very often wrong, and vice versa. Its
fundamental principle is the sale of securities to the public;
however, since the public has been more a seller than a
buyer for eight straight years, as measured by odd-lot activity, the average person might logically assume that there
soon will be no one ready to absorb any more stock.

Increasing amounts of this slack have gradually been
taken up by mutual funds and large institutional investors.
Only a few years ago they accounted for 50 percent of total
trading volume on the New York Stock Exchange; in the
mid seventies, institutions do about 75 percent of the business. Indeed, this business has become so vital to the lives
of most brokerage firms that many maintain special departments where tailor-made reports for institutional consumption are prepared.

Much of this information necessarily is derived from
the headquarters of the company about which the report

is written. Of course, the companies themselves are very pleased to be courted, especially if the report is favorable. They realize that virtually nothing improves confidence in a company and attracts buyers to its products more than being harnessed to a rapidly rising stock. The higher the price goes, the cheaper the costs of financing and the greater the value of its stock options.

The pride of management in bringing this about is an important factor too.

An entire profession has thus developed around the function of informing and influencing institutional investors. Take XYZ, for example, a dormant, do-nothing issue with a dull history. Perhaps new and aggressive management is about to take over, or some revolutionary product has been developed; a beneficial merger may be pending, or a spin-off of assets is in the works. In order to capitalize such developments, the company must sell itself to securities analysts. Just as nature adorns a bird with brilliant plumage to lure a mate, so must a company present itself in the brightest light possible to attract institutional attention.

Few experiences are more flattering, or disarming, to a securities analyst than to be flown to a company's headquarters by private jet to confer with its top officials. As an analyst for the Keystone Funds, I certainly was no exception when one day in 1968 at Boston's Logan Airport, a Jet Falcon landed to pick up five or six aerospace analysts, including myself, for a flight to Texas.

An impossible-to-refuse invitation had been received from a no-doubt gorgeous secretary who purred seductively into the phone: "Mr. LeBaron, won't y'all come down to Dallas and have dinner with Jim Ling? He'd like to tell you some of the things he's doing with LTV (Ling-Temco-Vought). As you are a large investor, it's important that he know your views."

Our party boarded the jet at Butler Terminal—noting that the copilot was Paul Thayer, president of LTV Aerospace—and took off for Texas, via Illinois. Jim Ling was in Illinois to dedicate a steel plant for Jones & Laughlin, which LTV had partially acquired. LTV was then a very aggressive conglomerate, having used debt, warrants, and preferred stock along with intricate accounting techniques, to create a multibillion-dollar empire.

Complex financial programs, designed to enhance the computation of reported earnings per share, were a typical hallmark of Ling, but in his quest for companies, he had been stymied suddenly by a lack of cash. In looking around for a means to offset this deficiency, Ling's gaze had fallen on cash-rich Jones & Laughlin. It seemed the answer to a prayer, for it could add immeasurably to his asset base.

Yet the acquisition proceedings were destined to travel a rocky road. The management of J & L was not cooperative. Like an overly bashful bride on her wedding night, it rebuffed the advances of the lanky Texan, who dressed habitually in grey slacks and dazzling tweed jackets. At the time of the Dallas conference, Ling had already exhausted his short-term borrowing ability to acquire J & L stock.

James Ling personified the popular idea of a corporate entrepreneur: tall and lean; a self-made millionaire, quick with figures. His money-making capacity seemed to rub off easily on close associates, and he had an instant grip on everyone connected with LTV. Most securities analysts liked him for his lack of formality.

Ling and Roscoe Haynie boarded the Falcon in Illinois. Haynie, the chairman of LTV's executive committee, was also a former chairman of Wilson & Company, which LTV had acquired several years earlier. He sat opposite me in the cabin; when drinks were served, he quickly dispatched several double scotches. I asked Roscoe what was troubling him, angling for an inside scoop on what was to come. However, I learned that the issue was not business or investment, but aeronautical.

Jim Ling occupied the captain's seat on the port side and was taxiing the jet out for takeoff. It was a hair-raising experience, which reminded me more of nervous reindeer trying to get airborne than anything connected with corporate aviation. Roscoe then confided that Jim had only four hours of dual instruction, all in a jet, and that he was not taking kindly to flying suggestions from the company's pilot in the adjacent seat. I had the fleeting thought that we may be in the hands of an egomaniac.

The jet landed at Dallas, after an unusually bumpy and eventful flight, and we were joined by a group of about a dozen investment managers pulled together from all over the country. Our hosts for the evening were the LTV management: Jim Ling, the board chairman; his main associates, Clyde Skeen and Roscoe Haynie; and three or four corporate officers. Dinner was served in a suite of offices at the top of the Tower. The moment it was over we filed into the Board Room, a large space decorated in the Spanish motif, where the heads of several animals shot on an African safari or at Ling's ranch in northern Texas stared down at us from the walls.

Ling immediately began one of his magnificent presentations. He explained that he would offer a package of securities—LTV Aerospace, LTV Electro-System, and certain Wilson companies—in exchange for common stock of the parent company, warrants, debentures, and a little cash. The package he would offer in a day or two had a market value approximating $150 million, compared with a price of about $100 million that he was asking the institutions to give in exchange.

There stood Jim Ling, blandly offering the institutions an opportunity to participate in each of the "Baby

Lings" at an obviously generous discount from market prices. The proposal seemed reasonable and rational, yet it was also very complex. Was there a hidden "gimmick"?

The usual questions were asked about the exact date of the offering, the total number of shares of each item to be outstanding, and so forth. Everyone was relaxed and friendly, until one analyst prodded the hornet's nest by asking how well Lehman Brothers and Goldman Sachs, LTV's investment bankers in New York, understood such a complex proposal. The question seemed to catch Ling temporarily off guard, but more likely it rubbed his most sensitive nerve. With the majesty of an iceberg and the tone of voice to match, he snapped back: "They understood a million dollars annually in fees and that's all they have to understand."

The mood of the gathering changed abruptly. Ling was no longer master of the situation, explaining carefully and patiently a complex problem to a receptive audience. The hunter and the quarry had suddenly changed places. Even certain institutions that had always been fans of Ling now balked at his proposal. The plan was little different from many others that succeeded; a mere exchange of paper was not the important stumbling block. It was the subterfuge! The cash that was to go from the institutions to LTV was relatively small. But, in this instance, it was essential, for LTV's coffers were virtually bare of funds.

The meeting concluded with both sides at loggerheads. The institutions had rebuffed Ling for the first time, yet still he insisted that the deal would go through. If they didn't accept it, individual investors would.

We left the hotel at eight o'clock the next morning for return flights to our respective cities. Just as the Boston plane was about to take off, I was summoned to the LTV pilot's room where Jim Ling waited on the phone. "Dean," he began, "I've now discovered that the deal has some tax problems. I wanted you to know that the exchange offer is not going to be made as planned and I'll let you know when we get something different. I suggest that you not mention this to anyone but, given your role of last evening, I thought you should have this information today." I thanked him for his hospitality and for keeping me informed. Five minutes later we were en route to Boston.

As one can imagine, I did not keep the information to myself. Since we were airborne during stock exchange trading hours, there was nothing any of us could act upon; however, at Logan Airport we learned that LTV had appreciated sharply in price that day. The other jets from Dallas had landed earlier than ours, and the participants of the meeting, believing that the exchange offer would take place and benefit Ling's cash position, had relayed this bullish information to their offices. Only we on the Boston plane knew the inside story.

Another company I visited as a securities analyst was Executive Jet Aviation, a separate but wholly owned subsidiary of Pennsylvania Railroad. E.J.A. wanted a member of the Keystone group (a speculative bond fund) to purchase a high-interest-rate mortgage on several aircraft in its corporate fleet. The deal included an equity kicker in the form of warrants, which might have considerable value at some future date. Keystone considered the idea intriguing and sent me and two other analysts to Columbus, Ohio, to check it out. My job was to write the report.

The two-hour meeting with E.J.A.'s officers and directors was the most unusual I ever attended. Former military brass was everywhere. Even the man who set up the projection screen was a retired lieutenant colonel. The gathering was friendly and informal, but I had no impression that many decisions were reached on the basis of the preliminary briefings by various E.J.A. officers. Apparently, the company relied upon its "big gun"—General Curtis

LeMay, the vice-chairman—to present most of the salient facts.

LeMay proposed immediately that E.J.A. buy a fleet of Lockheed C-5A's and enter the world air-cargo business. He rolled through the financing problems involved in buying these at $25 million apiece. He unfurled a chart giving ton-mile costs, which showed that air-freight costs contracted while other transportation forms expanded. Finally, he diagrammed a new terminal loading facility. One did not have to be clairvoyant to see that he wanted to put E.J.A. into the air-freight business in a big way.

It seemed quite natural, considering LeMay's military background and high position with E.J.A., that all of the company's internal procedures, repair forms, and the like would be modeled along the lines of Strategic Air Command. Indeed, the entire organization was a close facsimile of SAC. The setup seemed to confirm what I heard more than once during my visit.

When the time came that the nation needed more flying officers, as it surely would some day, E.J.A. would respond instantly as a fully functioning unit. The idea that such a need would ever arise again certainly was chilling. But I knew Curtis LeMay would be prepared. He had already advocated the bombing of any nation which exceeded certain limits of aggressive action as a means of preventing World War III.

The general concluded his presentation and opened the meeting to questions. Surprisingly, there were none. The audience was apparently satisfied that the company was following a normal and logical course. It had no specific problems, hence, there were no decisions to make. But, in my view, several of the proposals were quite revolutionary. I glanced at my Keystone associates who only smiled contentedly, so I decided to break the ice on my own. "Wouldn't it be better to lease these planes as the regulated air carriers do, rather than buying them at a huge expense to E.J.A.?" I asked General LeMay.

He rewarded me with a look, almost of surprise, as though I was the first person ever to ask him a direct question. Then he asked politely if I had been in the service. I replied that I had, and he wanted to know what rank I held. I said I was a corporal and heard loud groans around the room. The general pursed his lips and in a low voice replied that he did not answer questions posed to him by corporals.

He said it in such an offhanded way—as someone might refuse a cigarette by saying, "I don't smoke"—that I didn't believe he actually intended to be rude, but was merely stating a fact. Naturally, I felt put down and was embarrassed by the remark but, since there was nothing in my report that depended upon his answer, I simply shrugged off the incident and studied my notes.

On the way downtown to the Columbus Club where we were to be joined for lunch by other military people from the area—major generals predominating as it turned out later—I sat beside LeMay, who occupied the middle of the rear seat, puffing the habitual black cigar. I wondered if he was trying to further spell out his low opinion of a corporal's rank after a batch of his cigar ashes landed in my lap.

Our conversation in the car was very pleasant nonetheless. The general proved to be rather a charming and colorful luncheon companion, especially in describing his political aspirations and his consideration as a Republican presidential candidate in the 1968 primaries. Yet, in common with other people at SAC, LeMay had a rather odd streak.

"You know, Dean," he boomed across the table, "the reason we are working on Executive Jet is to prove to our civilian business friends that we are people who can make it also in 'civvies.' No one has said so directly to us, but we know that people who are not in the service think the only thing we can do is soldier. The military is the biggest business going. Our motives here are to show that it's no different in or out of uniform. It's still a business, and we know how to do it." I couldn't help wondering if his reference to uniforms included enlisted men. But since I was supposed to analyze the company and not the vice chairman, I made no comment.

E.J.A. was almost impossible to analyze by traditional methods. Probably its greatest asset was the backing by Pennsylvania Railroad. On the debit side, the leasing of jet time through use of its system was a brand new business, and one had to rely mainly upon intuition about the people involved. Moreover, the company appeared quite out of touch with reality; the chief legal counsel seemed the only officer with a level head.

I did not forecast in my report that the company would fail, but I did assert that any money invested there should be covered by something more tangible than the fortunes of Executive Jet. The warrants that came with it seemed devoid of any promise. But the collateral backing of a jet aircraft at 50 percent of market value appeared like good support for the loan which Keystone finally granted.

Executive Jet evolved into one of those "almost but not quite" companies. It had the potential of becoming a bonanza; unfortunately, it was only a puff of smoke. It barely survived alone and was a contributor to Penn-Central's demise in 1970. E.J.A. is still operative, but in a much lower key and only after a thorough financial overhaul.

The field of corporate financial relations is broad and complex. It involves much more than just trying to win analysts' approval of a merger, a new product, a change in management or a proposed exchange of securities for LTV or a mortgage for Executive Jet Aircraft.

Corporate officials are often looked upon as a source of numbers that may be used to sell investment committees and brokerage clients on the merits of a stock. Expressions like "in the ball park," or "it gives me a feel"—referring to an earnings estimate—do not actually violate the inside-information disclosure laws, but they do damage its spirit.

Following are certain pitfalls which analysts should guard against:

1. Some companies simply do not have good numbers, especially at critical turning points in the business. My first written analysis of a company included a guarded reference to quarterly figures that had been given me after the close of the accounting period but which I could not openly use. Imagine the shock I felt when the official numbers released two weeks later showed that my estimate, based on inside help, was 30 percent on the high side.

2. Analysts often tend to be overly friendly with management. They should be reminded that the investment-corporate relationship is basically antagonistic.

   The officers of a company naturally want its stock to sell at a high price. Potential investors, on the other hand, want it to sell at the lowest price possible, until they have bought it and become partners in the company. Their relationship thereafter is based almost entirely on the way the stock performs. Just as bankers who hoard money are the natural adversaries of builders who try to borrow it, so are investment analysts and corporate officials locked continually in competition for the public's dollar. An overly friendly attitude on the part of either one dulls the competitive spirit which is the pillar of their success. Both analysts and the companies involved must recognize that in the field of determining a correct price level for a security, their positions are not cooperative, but competitive.

3. An analyst's greatest mistake is asking the officer of a company for an opinion about its stock. Opinions so received should be ignored.

Corporate officials and directors obviously are the fountainheads of information about dividends, earnings, mergers, spin-offs, stock splits, acquisitions, and the like. Their opinions on such subjects are invariably worthwhile. Yet most directors and officers are poor judges of the stock market, particularly the prospects for their own company's stock. There is no dividing line between the forest and the trees. If a director owns the stock himself, he may be prejudiced about it. He is too close to the situation for his judgment to be the best.

When business is good, he is bullish on the stock; when business booms, he becomes ecstatic. But if sales start to slide and profit margins start to erode, or the stock zigs instead of zags within a gradually narrowing trading range, he may turn overly pessimistic. If he has sold some or all of his holdings prematurely, a similar condition will prevail. No one is more bearish than a sold-out bull! An officer or director may describe his company's future honestly and clearly as he sees it. But his glasses are too often clouded by personal prejudices.

4. Insider buying of a stock is a much more reliable barometer of the future than insider selling, especially in the case of new and smaller companies with relatively limited capitalizations. With large companies, little significance should be attached to insider activity.

   The founders or older officers may have acquired substantial stock positions over a period of time through stock splits or dividends or by exercising options. Any sales they make of the stock may be only for the purpose of putting their financial house in order to meet inheritance taxes later on. Moreover, their selling may be well absorbed or offset entirely through simultaneous purchases being made by newcomers to the company who are interested in the stock as long-term investment. Insider transactions involving large companies, such as IBM or General Motors, mean very little in terms of future market performance.

Communications between corporate management and the investment community are maintained on fine wires of nervous tension. The company wants to maintain its security at a high and stable price; the analyst wants to maintain a degree of controversy. He wants it to keep active —what some investors call a "turnstile stock"—one that is in the public eye with many buyers and sellers at all times.

Whereas the analyst will try constantly to uncover negative developments which might otherwise be surprising, the company will try to conceal any negative information. The analyst cannot expect to be told of bearish news in advance, but he must certainly establish and maintain a liaison with the company in order to stay abreast of developments—good or bad.

It is a sham to consider that the president of a company plans for future growth all the time. Often the chief executive spends his entire day dealing with problems. But he can take off his problem hat and put on his snow-job hat whenever an analyst comes to call. The analyst rarely asks the president, "How do you spend your day?" The analyst cannot expect a company to advise him in advance of surprise negative information. On the other hand, he must establish some sources if he is following the company for this type of input.

Competitors are useful sources of information. Sometimes junior members of management are very open. In fact, those who are most candid with the investment community are the senior or junior people. The middle group, with whom the analyst might have his greatest contact, is generally much too reserved and discreet.

Nearly all publicly owned companies have some program to influence the investment community to favor their stock. They hope that by so doing the market price will be higher than would otherwise be true, and investors will thereby do their part to provide the company with cheaper sources of equity capital. A high stock price is of course also good for management's ego and stock options. While there's some conjecture about the real value of such programs in markets such as we've had in the early seventies, I have a few suggestions.

As I've mentioned, there is nothing a company management can do to influence an investment analyst more than send the company plane for him. I once was picked up in Boston by a Gulfstream from American Can and flown in glorious splendor in back of the aircraft to Newark Airport where I was met by a limousine that wheeled out onto the apron, with the chauffeur opening his door as the ramp came down. That was heady stuff for a young analyst and, regardless of the dull outlook for American Can, they had won a friend through ego bribery. There was little that I could see the rest of the day that compared with my appreciation for the company's ability to treat me with proper respect.

The second activity that benefits a company is to call all analysts by their first names and to encourage the analyst to do likewise with the company officials. It is important for an analyst to feel "close to" the companies he follows. One example of this is his use of the first name for people who run the company, particularly where a single dynamic individual is at the helm. It is always useful to be on a familiar basis with famous or well-known people.

Introductions to politicians or movie stars are also ego-gratifying. Some brokerage houses for years have had programs where they bring in famous consultants for discussion on topics that are only remotely concerned with the investment field, but where the first-name basis is encouraged.

I met Dr. Henry Kissinger in his Harvard office, under the auspices of a brokerage-house consulting arrangement to discuss foreign affairs. Kissinger was quite famous at the time, although his only formal status was as foreign policy advisor to Governor Nelson Rockefeller. During the meeting, which ran from 8 P.M. to 11 P.M., a group of five investment people consumed Elsie's roast beef sandwiches, picked up from a famous eatery of that name in Harvard Square, and discussed Vietnam.

During that discussion, Kissinger went out of the room to arrange a telephone call to Secretary of Defense MacNamara in Vietnam. One had the feeling of being involved with major events; surely, this was well worth the commission dollars that this brokerage firm received. How it helped investment decision-making is a bit more obscure, but it certainly bolstered the confidence of young, inexperienced portfolio managers in dealing with large issues. It produced instant global maturity and may have well been worth the investment on those grounds.

Incidentally, Kissinger and other consultants are quite candid in these small groups. They recognize that their first job is to impress and to develop close associations, and their observations tend to be quite accurate. Kissinger, for example, commented—this was during the latter period of President Johnson's administration—that the Vietnam war was the wrong war, in the wrong place, being fought by the wrong people. So many mistakes were being made it was difficult to unscramble which was causing us the most problem. He suspected that we would have to negotiate our way out—a procedure which would be considered tantamount to defeat. On the other hand, it was just possible that the military bungling was sufficiently great that by correcting a few things on the ground, which would essentially increase the mobility and force on the north, we could win a military victory. This would be preferable for America's position in the world and its own morale, he felt, to having a nominal defeat.

In a sense he was hinting at the dual policy which we later followed of talking peace and waging war simultaneously. It was outstanding insight into policy which was to become dominant for the first four years of the Nixon administration.

Another activity which can benefit a company is to follow a policy of elitism. The company tries to develop a special relationship with a small group of analysts or investment people, usually from brokerage firms, on the basis of a greater sharing of information than would be customary—greater, in fact, than would be possible by law.

Many such analysts may be consulted on corporate dividend polices and asked to help with speech writing; in fact, they may be drawn within the company on a consulting basis. The analyst thus becomes "part of the family"—an ego-satisfying experience—especially for a young analyst who is then put on a more or less equal footing with the more mature executive. Few analysts can fail to respond favorably to such a situation.

I have helped companies write speeches, which gave me access to information prior to other investors. Once I was in a close working relationship with a large company in its early days. The president called me regularly to explain major corporate developments that were scheduled in coming weeks. I assumed these were just for information, until after several occasions he asked me: "Dean, are you making money for yourself on what I'm telling you?" I said, "Of course not, it wouldn't be ethical." He replied ,"Hell, why do you think I've been going to all this trouble?" In other words, he was attempting to pay me back for help I had been to the company in recommending the stock earlier.

The more freewheeling practices tended to go out of style in the late sixties. Today, analysts respond to companies which provide them with good industry statistics. One company even has a weekly recorded message for analysts on a toll-free phone. Usually there will be one company identified as the leader in its industry, and analysts will turn to the corporate financial people of this company for help in doing long industry reports. The analyst is interested in direct plagiarism and will accept company figures as his own. This is one of the things which establishes a close working relationship. It also usually increases the price/earnings ratio of the stock.

The company can, by design, elect to be aloof from Wall Street. There is no special evidence that this procedure backfires. Companies which have done so in many cases create a mystique. If their record is impeccable and the industry in which they operate has an aura of growth, aloofness may work as a strategy in maintaining a high price.

Whatever the relationship, both investors and companies must recognize that in the field of determining a correct price level for a security, they are in a competitive—not a cooperative—position.

2
The Role of
Academics,
Government, and
Brokers

Academics

I recently attended a luncheon in Boston with the heads of twenty of the largest and most respected investment firms. The speaker was Professor Robert Glauber who teaches investment management at the Harvard Business School. The average age of the guests was late sixties. Each one listened attentively to Bob Glauber, half their age, telling them that the markets were efficient in that there was no way they could select securities that would outperform the market and that marketing was the principal function of investment organizations. Here were executives—good salesmen too, as the heads of any investment organizations must be—listening to a young fellow tell them that the thing they thought they had spent their working lives doing was just a sham and that, to be honest, there wasn't much they could do that was better than the other fellow.

I considered it remarkable that these men attended the lunch in the first place; even more so to hear them take without rebuttal a line which should have been contentious. Certainly this type of lunch would never have taken place five years ago. Even if it were arranged just two years ago, it would have been poorly attended or several people would have walked out.

This lunch illustrates to me the acceptability of the academic in the investment world today. This acceptability is excessive and requires as much examination as the nonacceptance of the academic view ten years ago. Nearly every major institution has an academic or two on its consulting staff. Some of them are there for economic consulting. Others attend as management consultants to advise about the way the business should be run. Very few utilize this opportunity to be kept abreast of the large amount of securities research that is being done by academic institutions. Certainly no one to my knowledge in the institutional community is directing academic research along lines that are designed to find profitable investments or market imperfections.

The academic has a great influence on the investment business through his students. Many of those who join the professional staffs of large institutions have had business-school training at one of the graduate business schools in the country. There they are exposed to the leading teachers of investment management who espouse the primacy-of-marketing view. These young men have been coming into institutions for the last several years accepting the notion that professional service is difficult if not impossible.

The academic is the one who set this notion underway. Perhaps it was fueled at first by cynicism of the academic to the overpaid investment manager. Now the cynicism has a momentum of its own, aided by poor markets. The academic is in a leadership position and is well respected within the practicing institutional community. Few academics have been called upon to engage in long-range industrial planning, although it is a role for which they seem ideally suited.

Most academics I have known have had a hard time investing for their own account. There was an investment club of Harvard Business School professors in the 1960's which drew on the knowledge of about twenty senior faculty members. All of the input from consulting, case studies, and intelligence of the group was available for decision-making. The only investment that made any profit involved early purchase of stock in the Boston team of the American Football League. The students followed it to see if weekend game scores had any relationship to stock price.

My firm has made itself available for case studies and has maintained a close contact with academics. I find increasing disagreement with the implications of some of the views they hold. However, I have few disagreements with the sources of their observations. The academic community has been the principal leader in the use of quantitative techniques for investment decision-making.

As we have moved from qualitative judgments about securities and markets and acquired access to inexpensive but massive computer power, quantitative techniques for securities selection—essentially screening—have become practical. Few institutions realize that through the use of quantitative techniques they can run portfolios containing many more securities than were possible before.

There is no longer need to rely upon the few issues in a portfolio that one can follow by conventional techniques. The establishment of mechanical strategies, with automatic quantitative rules for purchases and sales, was spawned within the academic community through the research they did in the late sixties. By the late seventies, this research should be quite commonly employed for large institutional portfolios, with hundreds of securities followed by machine, where the portfolio manager generally establishes the criteria for selection or elimination, while the machine does the rest.

This major step will make a portfolio manager much more productive and will eliminate a great deal of the work and duplicate effort presently being done. It is the academic who is introducing quantitative discipline into investment operations.

Government

The government's role in the investment environment is ambivalent. Government seems to be dedicated to protecting the small investor at the sacrifice of the large investor and has not yet decided whether institutions are really a collection of small investors or a single large investor. Studies such as the Security and Exchange Commission's institutional study of the early seventies confuse more than they illuminate. The SEC's conclusion that institutions did not dominate the market is laughable on the surface. Anyone who has testified before the SEC in Washington comes away feeling convinced that the investor process is not understood. Well-meaning but inexperienced young lawyers are operating in an excessively complex and subtle field. Investment professionals can usually beat these people in any type of competition they may wish to undertake.

I have been at the SEC on several occasions and come away feeling sympathetic. Most of the work is done by young lawyers who are putting in a couple of years of internship before they go off to more lucrative work with law firms specializing in investment matters.

I was once called to testify in connection with possible institutional interference in the proposed merger of Brunswick and Union Tank Car. Brunswick was a quite leveraged growth company headquartered in Chicago.

Union Tank Car had a complementary financial structure whose management might have been the ultimate successor to the combined companies. Because Union Tank Car had a history of sharply lower rates-of-earnings growth, several investors in Brunswick were unenthusiastic about the merger prospects. The Investment Companies Act requires that mutual funds not participate in management decisions before being asked to vote on a corporate matter. The specific issue being investigated was whether or not Keystone had illegally influenced Brunswick against the merger by soliciting the opinions of other share holders of Brunswick.

This was a very difficult case to pin down. In conversations with the company and, indeed, over dinner one night with the Brunswick president, I expressed my views that the proposed merger was not in the best interests of shareholders. Keystone would vote against the merger. The issue was whether we had discussed our vote with other shareholders. The Boston investment community is quite small and it is not uncommon for institutions who own the same stock to exchange views and opinions or information about the company. Surely some such conversations took place on the Brunswick-Union matter, but there was no specific campaign to drum up support against the merger or specific calls for that purpose.

I spent a morning being questioned by an intelligent, intense young lawyer who had telephone logs of the company officials—an accurate description of what I had said to the company. He was looking for evidence of specific conversations with other institutions in which I might have tried to influence their decision for or against the merger. Though I could not think then, or now, of any specific conversations, it was reasonable for some to have occurred. Indeed, they would have been commonplace.

There have been proposals that government legislate the capital allocation process. Institutional investors tend to favor the large and historically successful companies and leave the smaller, harder-to-follow ones alone. The cost of equity capital for smaller companies is much higher as a result, and serious consideration is being given to the idea that large investors, primarily banks, might be required to invest a portion of their funds in a selection of smaller company stocks. If such a law came about, it would be a subtle form of capital tax and would defeat the notion that capital is attracted to investments where it can get the highest return commensurate with risk.

Government is clearly going to have a much bigger role in the investment process than was formerly the case. Tax-exempt funds, like pension plans and foundations, must apply annually for tax-exempt status. Someday, a legislator is going to decide that those funds can be allocated by government fiat without passing new tax laws. The securities industry has a tradition of self-regulation which has been proven faulty. Government will assume these burdens.

Proposals have been made for a Federal Securities Exchange like the Federal Reserve System, but for stocks and bonds rather than check clearance. Such proposals have great merit and indicate, since they must come from government, how backward is self-initiated change in this field. In a sense, there is little reason to differentiate between bank deposits and equities. They are different forms of capital but can logically be treated within the same system.

Brokers

The typical individual investor expects too much from his broker, and the broker lives out this fantasy by recommending stock that, he claims, will produce great profit instantly. In fact, in the new-issue crazes which come near the end of every bull market, the broker is the conduit through which the individual investor gets instant profit. It is the case unfortunately that the investor usually ends up with losses on the new issues after the bull market tops out.

Institutions, on the other hand, expect too little from brokers. They are not demanding enough for the huge commission flow for which they are responsible. In the year in which Keystone's brokerage commissions totaled slightly over $20 million, half went for investment services. These are the so-called soft dollars which are used to designate money owned by and spent for the ultimate client. Brokerage firms often act as conversion agents of soft dollars (commissions) into hard dollars (money spent to hire consultants to do research and the like). The conversion rate between soft dollars and hard dollars used to be as high as five to one, but in the tight markets of 1974 it was running at approximately two to one.

Because the demands were too little in the post-May 1, 1975 negotiated rate environment, institutions were ruthless in driving charges down 50 percent and in seeking a price appropriate to the value for services rendered. Had demands for better services been made earlier, and they would have been if the institutions had been spending their own money on commissions, the cuts would have been tempered.

The principal motivation of a broker is sales. His task is to sense what his clients want to buy or sell and provide them with valid reasons for doing so. When I took over the operation of a large fund, I noticed that most brokers would tell me how brilliant I was to own the stocks I already held in the portfolio. They promised their organizations would follow these very closely for me. I found few suggestions or new ideas and almost none that could be classed as controversial.

Indeed, I was attracted to these brokers; they had the same investment style I was pursuing. I rewarded them with large commissions which invariably brought them back to tell me again how good the portfolio was. This helped the broker's pocketbook but it added little I might learn about the portfolio nor brought out other things I should be pursuing.

Brokers are aggressive salesmen but very conservative investors. They have learned that it is safest to operate with the consensus, to be noncontroversial, and not to expect too much in the way of sharply above-average or sharply below-average results. When brokers are placed on a board of directors, they become the most cautious members and shun high business risks. Even the brokerage business itself, beset by problems as it is, has suffered because of its inability to change. Brokers are far better at raising capital for older ventures than for newer ones. Very few, for example, have become leaders in venture capital. Instead, the insurance companies—by reputation even more conservative investors than brokers—have held the leadership position.

The principal service one can expect from brokers is gossip. Certainly this is not widely advertised, nor is it even understood by investors. The brokering and sales functions come in contact with many investors during the day to the extent that the broker is attracted to those with the most commission dollars; consequently, those who are currently most active in the market. His contact is weighted toward people who are most responsible for affecting current market prices.

If a broker is an accurate observer (and most are), he can be expected to provide an instant polling of investor attitudes; gossip on changes in favoritism, personnel, different industries, or companies; and even information on which investment strategies are working. Most brokers would put the traditional small-town telephone operator to shame as sources of community information. Much of the evidence that the market is efficiently priced is attributable to the successful gossip function of brokers. They are constantly evening out pricing imperfections. Brokers can be expected to enjoy displaying how well connected they are with the largest customers, and a little bit of flattery will extract all of the information one might want. Most brokers do not realize how important this gossip function can be to an investor; they do not even think that it is very highly prized. It usually can be extracted as part of the social interaction between a broker and an investor, rather than as a specific service being provided for commission dollars.

Brokers are caught in the dilemma of having a service which is priced higher than the level necessary to support a specific security execution. By tradition, the execution service is relatively undifferentiated and can be effected by any one of hundreds of brokers. In order to attract customers, brokers have added analytical, economic, and even culinary services for their principal accounts in order to attract the business which will contribute so importantly to their overhead.

There are probably few industries where so much general information is available as the investment business. Brokerage reports and masses of statistical data are provided free or at very low cost, but few know how to use this resource. In fact, few people in the investment business as a whole have the faintest idea what sort of information works and what does not work.

One of the principal activities of a brokerage research department is to forecast earnings per share for companies which they, like other research departments, follow. The technique most widely employed by an analyst is to call the company in question. A fishing conversation will occur with the company executive being asked to accept an estimated figure. The analyst will then fill in some assumptions on a pro forma income statement to show how this result comes about and present it as original work. There is ample evidence that earnings per share forecasts are not very good and even when accurate they have already been discounted in the marketplace. They are not very profitable exercises, although hundreds of millions of dollars are spent by brokers in this activity.

Perhaps a broker performs a ceremonial function for investors. Frequently a customer asks his broker if it was all right to buy some particular stock. The broker replies, "Yes, I have checked with our research department and they say it is." A ceremonial exchange is taking place to give the customer confidence that a decision involving large sums with a high uncertainty of success is likely to be correct. One goes to the high priest who offers a few mumbo-jumbo words to the investment gods. The priests extract a high tax for this service. And the investor leaves the broker's office assured that his investment progress will be bountiful because the proper oracles were consulted.

Brokers provide good training to investors, whether institutional or individual. Several days spent in the brokerage operation gives one an insight into the activities of other investors. The contrast between the pace in the trading room with much frantic activity and the calm reflection of the corporate finance department suggests totally different business attitudes. Brokers have little desire to plan in their own business. Not only are they traditionally capital short because they distribute profits each year, but the business is usually tied to the activities of the few individuals rather than to a continuing corporate entity.

Two weeks after I was first employed by F. S. Moseley & Co., I submitted a planning report and the observations I had made about brokerage houses during the interview process at the Harvard Business School. I felt that these observations would be useful insights in the determination of overall firm policy, and perhaps I also hoped that it would win a place for me in the high planning councils of the firm I had joined.

The seventy-year-old managing partner, John O. Stubbs, took one look at the outline which I had carefully prepared and handed it back with a look which put me in my whippersnapper place and said, "The only thing you have to remember here is to sell stock to anyone who has money. The only reason I wanted a research department is because our largest customer says it's a good thing to have. Our largest customer wants to do business with us anyway and needs an excuse. I don't think you fellows can pick stocks any more than anyone else and certainly I don't need you. But if every other major firm is going to have a research department, I guess we have to and it had better be a damn good one."

I was set back on my heels, yet I learned a clear expression of the essence of the brokerage firm behind its genteel facade. I learned early that it really moves on sales and I structured the research department to sell directly to institutions. I also developed a reasonably large personal brokerage clientele myself. Any administrator in the brokerage field who does not control any commission business is the first to be chopped in a cutback.

A broker is always dealing with divided loyalties and conflicts of interest. He can always be expected to select the alternative which offers him the highest and most stable return. An obvious conflict is between corporate finance clients and brokerage clients. When a brokerage firm has an underwriting, it prices the issue at a price that will sell. Part of the selling process, however, is the reputation of the investment firm and its ability to continue to follow a security and to provide information (or at least ceremonial services) which make investors think the company is still a good one. Further, it creates the impression that any problems are only temporary, and these will be overcome by the extraordinary skill of management.

A glaring example of this conflict occurred when I was asked to visit one of F. S. Moseley's corporate finance clients—Sprague Electric—at a time when the stock was down, and the company was particularly insistent about getting some support for its falling stock price. The company was nearby and was in a field I knew quite well. I welcomed the opportunity to spend a day meeting with the top people.

Everything I learned from the company visit suggested that the electronics business was in a very bad way; Sprague worse than most. Its business, passive components, was being made obsolete by integrated circuits, in which it was not a leader. Selling prices were coming down and costs were going up. There was little good about the situation, except that Sprague was an old and stable New England company that probably would weather this temporary condition as it had many others. The company was very honest about its difficulties and a number of the management people I met were quite candid in explaining the problems. After all, I represented the underwriter and was considered one of the family.

I returned to the office and wrote a sale recommendation on the company. I sent the draft directly to Sprague's chairman for his comment and review before it was to be sent out to customers. When the managing partner came in the next day, I heard some thundering about writing a sale recommendation rather than a buy recommendation on the firm's pet company. He roared that I must have misunderstood the purpose of my visit and, thank heavens, that my report didn't get out to the public. There was no question that I had violated one of the principal rules of the firm: you never dislike one of your own underwritings. Clearly this report never saw the light of day and our clients went uninformed about the business problems at Sprague.

Instead, a bland information memo was issued which didn't say very much but satisfied nearly everyone. It contained some historical statistical information and gave the impression to Sprague that F. S. Moseley was indeed doing its part in following the stock. The clients could read into it that, after all, the firm wouldn't be putting out a report if it felt things weren't going pretty well, and I was satisfied that I had not published the requested buy recommendation. The problem was that the report did not accomplish any useful purpose in giving someone investment guidance.

Institutional investors dominate the commission structure. About $7 billion is spent annually in commissions and investment fees, the bulk of which is in commissions related to transactions. Large institutional investors with perhaps $200 billion in assets have replaced the wealthy individual as the chief source of income for most brokers. The power to direct commissions and transactions, far greater than was held by the legendary robber barons of the past, is now in the hands of fairly junior institutional employees. They will reward brokers for a multiplicity of services, some obvious and some subtle.

Stories abound of liquor and girls being used to attract commissions. It must be a sad commentary on my image that offers of that nature have never been made to me, and I am unable to report some of the sexier sides of the investment activity.

I have mentioned that brokers tend to pander institutions by complimenting them on things which the institution has already done. Moreover, the trend of communication between broker and institution has changed tremendously and such change reflects structural shifts within the business itself.

As institutional investors became more intense, performance-oriented, and less conservative with capital during the fifties, a new type of broker was spawned. The archetype institutional firm was pioneered by Donaldson, Lufkin, and Jenrette—three bright, young, well-experienced Harvard Business School graduates. Their contribution to the evolution of investment practice was the development of in-depth reports on unusually attractive industries and companies; typically companies large enough to be attractive to many institutional investors simultaneously but companies that were not exclusively big.

They would claim to have more knowledge of that company or industry than anyone else. They went well beyond the demands of many investors at that time, which were only for information that was contained in a company's annual report and a Standard & Poor's tear sheet. After all, how much information did one need to supplement a large institution's knowledge of IBM, Standard Oil of New Jersey (later Exxon), or General Motors?

There was a growing need for such information and DLJ capitalized on this requirement. The companies they sponsored and followed prospered during the last third of the bull market, while the company itself prospered for its innovative activities. They pioneered the brokerage report of fifty to a hundred pages, which could be used as a file document giving evidence that the institutional investor had prudently examined the investment alternative far more than he could have by any other service. In effect, DLJ fired at their target companies with a high-powered rifle equipped with telescopic sights rather than blazing away with a shotgun at anything that moved. The information was persuasively presented, well documented, and provided both depth and breadth to a fundamentally oriented investment decision. Dozens of firms imitated this practice and many succeeded in establishing, for themselves at least, an equal place in the eyes of institutions for in-depth service.

As the pace of the market quickened from the mid sixties, the time required to thoroughly research, document, and distribute detailed information proved inadequate for performance-hungry institutions. Increasingly, results had to be conveyed to institutional investors before the final report was completed. While it was being prepared, brief summaries of recommendations would be disseminated, or salesmen who maintained a close contact with their own research department would verbally convey the information that was to come later in the full-dress report.

The recipients of the advance word were consciously aware that future buyers, on the basis of the tailor-made report, would push the price up or that institutional investors would buy on the sketchier advance information. What actually happened was that information demands receded to the point at which commitments would be made, with some understanding that insurance for success would appear later in the form of a more detailed report that would spark buying pressure from the slower-moving institutional investors.

The individual investor, meanwhile, was caught in the backwash of both vessels. Not only did most brokerage firms separate their research departments into two groups—institutional and retail (with the better analysts going to the institutional area)—but it was general practice for retail analysts to pick up ideas from the institutional analysts after they were discarded or exploited. The retail analyst would get sufficient documentation presumably to attract a retail customer. Evidence of a rising stock price would be part of the documentation that the idea was good for a retail buyer. This early start would have been created by initial moves of the aggressive institutional investors.

This situation was the "greater fool" theory in action. Three levels of investors were being served by the institutional broker: the institutional investor who would move on sketchy advance warning knowing that a report was to come; the institutional investor who required the detailed report—often a bank or trust company that would find it difficult to add a new name; and the retail customer at the end of the line.

This practice was effective in the mid to late sixties when the bull market topped out in an orgy of speculation and new issues that ended in 1967. The volatile markets that have ensued since then, where the Dow Jones Industrial Average has ranged between 600 and 1,000 and the average price decline on the New York Stock Exchange has been more volatile—falling about 70 percent, have created a different character.

Brokerage firms no longer tout the performance record of their recommendations and the likelihood that they will produce instant or ultimate success. The move by brokerage research departments to institutions has been in the direction not of recommendations but of "service." We have had the phenomenon created throughout the late sixties and early seventies of the so-called one-decision stock—a security of superlative quality and persistent earnings growth that one wished to hold perpetually. Since all brokers and institutions can identify these privileged securities, there really is no point in recreating long, detailed reports that delve into the history and industry structure of, for example, some of the leading drug companies. This work has already been done so many times that it has been accepted for many years as being redundant. If the names that institutions wish to have in their portfolios are known, what can a brokerage firm do to attract commissions from large institutional shareholders?

Within the notion of service comes the objective of closely following a security, that is, reporting corporate events more quickly than other people. This may not be directed toward specific transactions, buy or sell, on that paricular security. Rather, the reporting of events allows the institutional analyst or portfolio manager to appear well informed. To the extent that portfolio and stock price changes may be at least random for highly institutionalized securities, the timely knowledge of company news may serve one's own career. There should be no surprises in a portfolio so that price changes can be ascribed to outside environmental forces, not to analytical sloppiness. Service, then, is not necessarily directed toward building portfolios that are more profitable, rather it is built around protecting the job interests of the individual who distributes the commissions.

To the extent that the allocation of commissions also supports the job security of the people in the brokerage firm, one has the impression of a business alliance for convenience. Of course, the only sufferer is the client who may be paying high management fees and commissions for activities that are not related to decisions that will favorably influence his profits.

There is a wide variety of brokerage reports and services available to institutions. At the more expensive level of service are consultations with economists, technicians, and political observers. These establish the general scene from which investment decisions will be made. Most institutional portfolio managers have now repudiated the value of stock selection and feel that the only things which are going to affect their results are the macrointerests of whether or not to be in the market and, if so, in what sector.

Stock selection can take care of itself through junior people in the organization or, for that matter, it may be taken at random. This proposition is valid only as long as all investors emphasize stock selection. Securities may be very closely and accurately priced by other investors. It is possible to plagiarize the stock-selection techniques of others by merely accepting today's price on the securities one wishes to buy or sell.

The next level of service by a broker for institutions

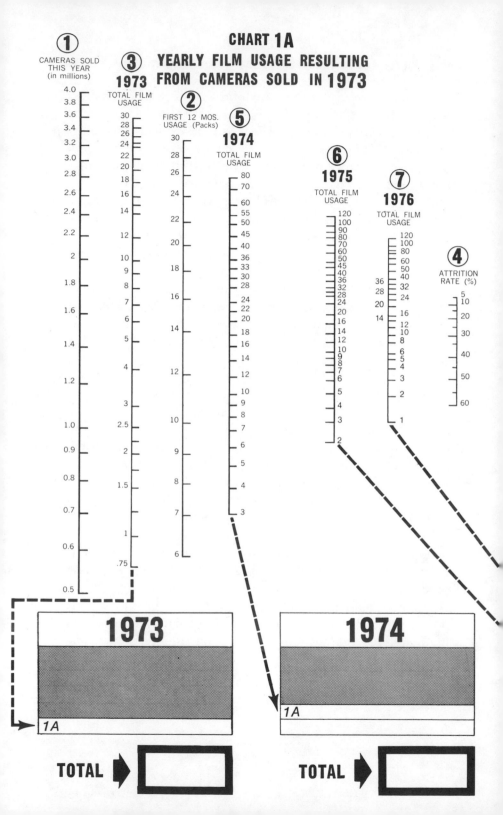

CHART 1A
YEARLY FILM USAGE RESULTING FROM CAMERAS SOLD IN 1973

① CAMERAS SOLD THIS YEAR (in millions)

③ 1973 TOTAL FILM USAGE

② FIRST 12 MOS. USAGE (Packs)

⑤ 1974 TOTAL FILM USAGE

⑥ 1975 TOTAL FILM USAGE

⑦ 1976 TOTAL FILM USAGE

④ ATTRITION RATE (%)

1973

1974

TOTAL

TOTAL

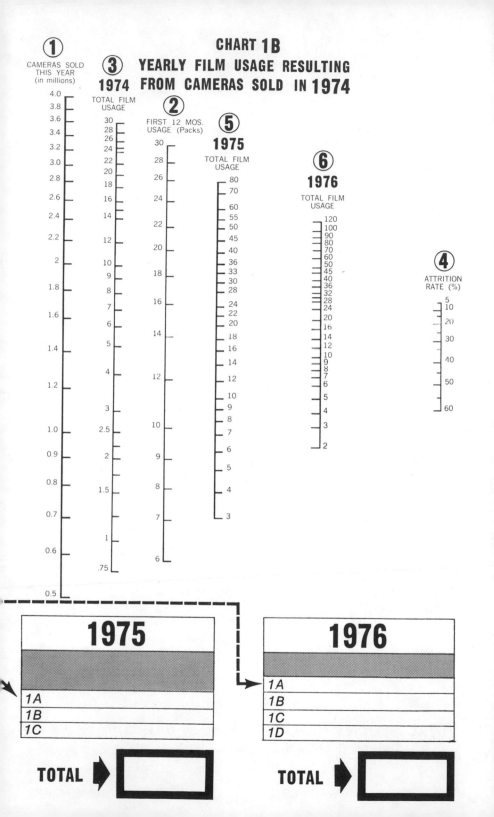

CHART 1B
YEARLY FILM USAGE RESULTING FROM CAMERAS SOLD IN 1974

CHART 1C
YEARLY FILM USAGE RESULTING
FROM CAMERAS SOLD IN 1975

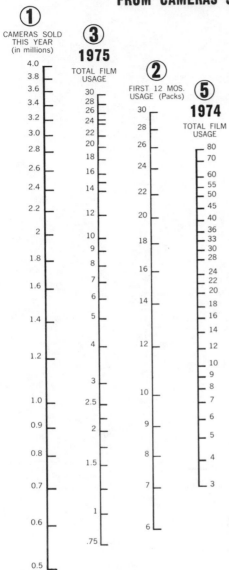

① CAMERAS SOLD
THIS YEAR
(in millions)

4.0
3.8
3.6
3.4
3.2
3.0
2.8
2.6
2.4
2.2
2
1.8
1.6
1.4
1.2
1.0
0.9
0.8
0.7
0.6
0.5

③ 1975
TOTAL FILM
USAGE

30
28
26
24
22
20
18
16
14
12
10
9
8
7
6
5
4
3
2.5
2
1.5
1
.75

② FIRST 12 MOS.
USAGE (Packs)

30
28
26
24
22
20
18
16
14
12
10
9
8
7
6

⑤ 1974
TOTAL FILM
USAGE

80
70
60
55
50
45
40
36
33
30
28
24
22
20
18
16
14
12
10
9
8
7
6
5
4
3

④ ATTRITION
RATE (%)

5
10
20
30
40
50
60

TOTAL INDICATES TOTAL FILM USAGE IN MILLION OF PACKS FOR
THE YEAR SHOWN.

CHART 1D
YEARLY FILM USAGE RESULTING
FROM CAMERAS SOLD IN 1976

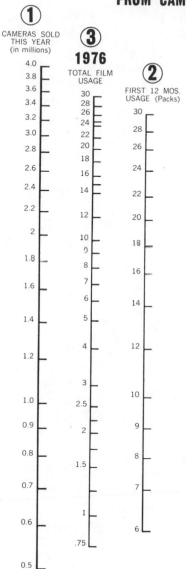

①
CAMERAS SOLD
THIS YEAR
(in millions)

- 4.0
- 3.8
- 3.6
- 3.4
- 3.2
- 3.0
- 2.8
- 2.6
- 2.4
- 2.2
- 2
- 1.8
- 1.6
- 1.4
- 1.2
- 1.0
- 0.9
- 0.8
- 0.7
- 0.6
- 0.5

③
1976
TOTAL FILM
USAGE

- 30
- 28
- 26
- 24
- 22
- 20
- 18
- 16
- 14
- 12
- 10
- 9
- 8
- 7
- 6
- 5
- 4
- 3
- 2.5
- 2
- 1.5
- 1
- .75

②
FIRST 12 MOS.
USAGE (Packs)

- 30
- 28
- 26
- 24
- 22
- 20
- 18
- 16
- 14
- 12
- 10
- 9
- 8
- 7
- 6

will be to have the best, or nearly the best, analyst for a particular industry. Nearly all institutions want to have access to industry specialists.

The best type of brokerage report, in my view, for an institution is that which identifies the critical variables in a technical or fundamental decision and assigns weights to these variables (in such a way that the institutional analyst decision-maker can change the weights if he wishes) and shows the conclusion that the brokerage analyst reaches and how he gets there.

A report prepared on Polaroid in 1972 by E. F. Hutton & Co. was one of the best I have seen on the company, yet it did not contain a single narrative word. This report (Figure 1, pp. 36–9) isolates the critical ingredients to determine Polaroid's profitability.

INSTRUCTIONS FOR CHARTS

1. Select values for the items listed on the Work Sheet and note them under the appropriate years.
2. CHART 1A—Draw a straight line connecting projected 1973 Aladdin Camera Sales ① and First-Year Usage ②. The intersection with vertical line ③ is connected with the Attrition Rate ④ by a straight line. Film Sales (in millions of packs) resulting from 1973 Camera Sales for the calendar years 1973–1976 may be read off this line where it intersects the appropriately marked vertical lines ③, ⑤, ⑥ and ⑦. These figures should be noted in boxes below the Chart as shown by the heavy dashed lines.
3. Repeat Step 2 for Charts 1B through 1D. Note calendar-year Total Film Usage figures in the appropriately marked boxes. Add the figures. The "TOTAL" shows film pack sales in millions of each calendar year.
4. CHART 2—*Aladdin Camera Sales*—Draw a straight line connecting Cameras Sold this year ① with the Average

Dealer Price per camera ②. The intersection with vertical scale ③ will give Revenue derived from camera sales. Connect that point with expected Operating Margin ④. The intersection with line ⑤ directly gives Earnings per Share resulting from camera sales. Note the figure in the box below the Chart.

5. CHART 3—*Aladdin Film Sales*—Total Film Sales for any year is obtained from the boxes accompanying Charts 1A, 1B, 1C, and 1D. Use this total figure on Chart 3, Line ①. Connect with anticipated Operating Margin ② to obtain Earnings per Share derived from total film sales ③. Note figure in box.

6. CHART 4—*Impact of Kodak on the Type 108 Market*—If you expect Kodak to be competing for the conventional Polaroid film market (Type 108/88) during the year under examination, connect Total Market Size (Type 108/88 film only) ① with the Market Share expected to be taken by Kodak ②. Line ③ will provide Earnings per share of market. If you do not anticipate Kodak's market entry, use 0% for the Eastman Kodak share to obtain Polaroid's earnings on its conventional film product. Note the figure in the box.

7. Add together the three boxed figures to obtain total Polaroid Earnings per Share for the year under consideration. An additional 40-50 cents per share, resulting from non-amateur activities and interest income, may be added to obtain total corporate earnings.

Since nearly everyone studying Polaroid has his own ideas as to pack usage per year and number of camera sales in different price brackets, building up the income statement becomes an exercise in which anyone can plug in his own estimates and relate them to the various stages of fixed and variable costs.

The other type of brokerage report, which receives

far more publicity, is the sell report of an institutional favorite—most likely caused by an earnings estimate reduction, by an analyst who has been closely identified with the security. The sharp price declines of institutional favorites like Polaroid, are often caused in the short run by this falling from favor with analysts or brokerage houses which have been strongly identified as the critical sources for information.

When a company from which a great deal is expected produces a down quarter in earnings or announces that earnings will be disappointing, a stock like Polaroid or Avon can rather quickly fall to a price 50 percent or more below former levels. Fortunately, many individual investors are not involved with these securities. It is mostly an institutional game where the volatility risks are understood.

Understanding risks and accepting their consequences are two entirely different judgments. Being responsible for an institutional portfolio that contains a number of institutionalized favorites and watching them go one by one in the midst of the late stages of a bear market to levels that have not been seen for many years is an experience in suffocation that is difficult to relate. One may rationalize that they deserve to be sold at any price, thereby removing the source of the pain. Such a mental attitude sets the scene for the classical panic liquidation which we all know often characterizes the final stages of many market declines.

3
Security Selection

The Efficient Market

There is a mountain of evidence that the stock market is efficient, that is, that prices accurately reflect a balanced judgment of all known facts about markets and particular securities. In the mid sixties when the "Random Walk" first challenged institutional investors, their response was to ignore the evidence. Academics had no following at that time. After all, in the twenty-five-year bull market to 1966, many people had made great fortunes in the equity markets. Why should one listen to a teacher who obviously had not made his fortune in the several decades of a good stock market?

If one examined the data when presented in the mid-sixties, one accepted the hypothesis that markets generally were efficient. After adjustment for volatility, there were few, if any, investors who systematically could produce returns above that which could have been achieved by chance. Furthermore, performance figures on institutional investors—essentially the more readily available mutual funds—were not predictive of future success. The entire notion of selecting mutual funds based upon past performance data being predictive was faulty.

Institutions should have accepted this academic challenge but gradually the notion that markets were efficient became widely accepted by institutional investors. At the present time, institutional investors among themselves admit that they cannot beat the market with large sums of money. They seem today to be even stronger adherents of the efficient-market hypothesis than academics. The strong form of the efficient-market hypothesis claims that securities are accurately priced at all times, reflecting the balance-of-judgment about the information that is available at any given time on the expected outcomes that will affect equities. Many institutional investors operate on this hypothesis today, providing client services in the form of risk adjustments and other handholding supplanting their earlier stress on portfolio construction and stock picking.

The weak form of the efficient-market hypothesis says that there may be imperfections in security pricing, but that these are too expensive for most institutional investors to exploit. From this weak form, we can derive a restatement for shaping investment policy.

It is possible to diagram the market (Figure 2) showing the tendency of individual securities toward something called normal value on any given day. This is based upon the natural force of potential buyers and sellers who withhold their potential action from the marketplace because they are not attracted to making transactions at a given price. A more customarily understood function is through active buyers and sellers operating at the margin. The spread around normal value is wider for securities of smaller market capitalization. Markets in the area of less capitalization

Figure 2

EFFICIENT MARKET SCHEMATIC

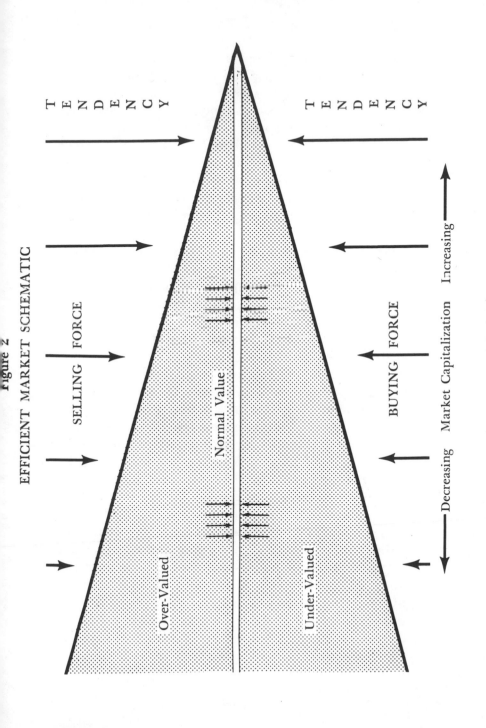

are not so efficient because the institutional investors who are dominating the pricing mechanism cannot operate conveniently with the same historic techniques they have used in thin markets. Size is an important determinant based upon ease of institutionalization, but there can be other characteristics as well—mundane industries, a geographic bias, and even a bias according to certain days of the calendar for different security universe subsets.

The inefficiently priced security can be analogous to the half-life of an artificially created element. When exposed to natural conditions, it tends to decay toward a stable condition quite rapidly. All of the laboratory measurement problems of artificially created elements are present in measuring the existence of imperfectly priced securities. The more time one expends to uncover inefficiently priced securities, the more likely the examiner is to find one whose half-life has decayed to the point where it approximates an efficiently priced security.

The theory of security pricing may be generally stated: the more accessible a security is to institutional investors, the more likely it is to be correctly priced in relation to similar securities. The entire universe from which the security may be drawn may not be correctly priced vis-à-vis all securities. The difficulty in exploiting market imperfections is inversely proportional to the incidence of institutional acceptance characteristics. Time erodes imperfect pricing without any investment action.

The investment process deals with allocation of capital, which is, in a sense, the promise of future goods and services that will be provided—modified to the extent that promises can be broken because they are inconvenient. The rights of capital, be they to pollute or infringe upon rights of others, can shrink without any transactions taking place to increase or decrease their value. Without the strength of law or precedent to enforce previously made business deal-

ings, capital does not exist. It is not the repository of something—like oil or a building. It merely represents a promise
that the proceeds from such things will be allocated according to a prescribed plan.

When the allocation is not in force, the capital ceases
to exist; and when the allocation of capital is limited,
it bears a shrinkage. Today, we say we are capital short,
meaning that many of the projects which should be undertaken involve large expenditures of capital. The only way in
which we can have capital is to forego expenditures for current goods and services; capital is the expectation that future goods and services will be paid back with some return.
In an inflationary environment this becomes more difficult,
since future capital is systematically eroded. Part of the
shortage, in my view, comes about from erosion of the force
of promises rather than from excessive demand for capital.
But, essentially, you have both things taking place. Because
of inflation and a world which has undergone a rapid economic transformation, the demand for capital is high and,
because of changes in the force of promises, the supply of
capital (promises) is lower.

Selection Techniques

Stock selection techniques are basically in two forms:
top-down and bottom-up. The top-down approach involves
beginning with an analysis of the overall economic environment, then narrowing to industries which may be especially
favored and, finally, selecting companies within an industry
which will be head and shoulders above other companies in
the same industry. Portfolio weightings can be arbitrarily set
as stronger or weaker than weightings in a popularly used
market index, such as Standard & Poor's 500.

The bottom-up approach ignores industry divisions
of the market and looks for those few places where the pricing may be imperfect, which for some reason has slipped the

attention of investors. It attempts to uncover underpriced securities, which, it is presumed, are likely to appreciate more in value than the market in general. Each security in effect is ranked against the entire market, rather than against a narrower universe of its own industry or other category.

Analysts tend to pursue the bottom-up approach, while portfolio managers favor the top-down. Although institutions can be segregated as favoring one over another, it is better, in my opinion, to run both techniques in parallel. Where a given investment opportunity satisfies the criteria of both techniques, one may be doubly encouraged by the likelihood of profit, since one technique confirms the other.

Within both approaches rests the opportunity to utilize fundamental and technical analysis. Fundamental analysis involves studies of the economy and of corporate enterprises that relate to earnings, assets, sales, and dividends; indeed, all activity which relates to securities analysis, but only in relation to what a company does and the currently prevailing price for its security. This analysis utilizes the marketplace as a single slice in time. The only information purpose of past price action is to establish price norms and not trends. There is a judgment that undervalued securities tend to move toward a higher normal value, and securities which are overvalued tend to move downward to a more normal value.

Technical analysis, on the other hand, concerns itself entirely with market price trends. In a sense it presumes the market is relatively perfect, and that the judgment of investors is revealed in pricing. It seems logical that there would be information content in price trends. Although statistical support for technical techniques is lacking, there is evidence that technical tools in the hands of a skilled technician add to the decision process. Price trends have a persistency and are occasionally revealed by recurring technical patterns. Some investors, particularly short-term traders, rely entirely upon technical studies as the patience required for the unfolding of fundamental value in the marketplace may be too great.

Again, my own preference is for a blending of both approaches, with fundamental input given a very high weight at all times and technical information being given a moderate weight in decision-making at critical turning points. In general, it may be said that fundamental analysis claims it is the best investment tool for determining *what* to buy or sell; technical analysis portends superiority for targeting the moment *when*!

One of the most difficult tasks an investor has in stock selection is his judgment and analysis of management capability. Large institutional investors consider that their junior people have the skills to analyze management talents, motivations, goals, and aspirations on the basis of intensive interviews. Most young analysts, however, do not have the investment background to undertake this task. Nor can they always relate well to the life styles and demands of those they are attempting to analyze. They can, on the other hand, be the subjects of excessive sales zeal by an excessively articulate management, with smoothness and salesmanship being taken as mistaken substitutes for objectivity and drive.

Other analysts feel that management skills, whatever they may be, are revealed in published accounting information. Income statement, balance sheet, and growth adequately testify to the presence of management skill. Although luck may be involved, the likelihood that it will be a causal factor for good corporate figures is reduced to a low level in a period of at least five years.

Corporate accounting is sufficiently loose and generally not responsive to immediate change. Accounting figures can hide company deterioration for a long period of time. Several examples come to mind. We had invested in an in-

surance company where the level of profitability had deteri-
orated steadily for five years, although adjusted earnings
rose in excess of 10 percent annually. The company had
been using its reserves, which were tucked in the corner of
various accounts in each of those years—assuming that each
subsequent year would allow a build-up of the reserve account. This company was eventually sold to a larger insurance company which makes a specialty of cleaning up sick
situations.

Another company we were involved in had the best
operating figures in its industry. It was founded and dominated by one man. When he died, he left control of the company evenly balanced between two sons-in-law and a son.
For a while there was no change in the company's progress.
The policies of the father continued until there was rapid
deterioration as the younger generation lost control of some
of the subsidiaries. Hard feelings resulted, and the company
became only a mild reflection of its former strength.

One of the most flagrant examples of the inadequacy
of accounting figures was a printing-machine company
working three shifts a day shipping machines to an unconsolidated leasing subsidiary across the street. R. Hoe's ware-
house was full of unsold equipment. Managements resort to
these expediencies only very rarely; they cannot remain in
effect for very long.

One problem with numbers in analyzing companies is
that they may lag. At best they are coincident and hardly ever
do they lead. One cannot use numbers as a guide for stock
selection except in a universe so neglected by investors that
stock prices lag fundamental changes. In a closely followed
universe like most institutionalized securities, numbers may
be inadequate. The numbers themselves fall behind changes
that have taken place within the company. Moreover, there
is intense competition among the numerous brokers and in-

stitutions who follow the securities and try to act ahead of the changes. The investor making a decision after numbers have been published for a closely studied universe will lag.

And yet, "number crunching" among analysts for large institutions is a most common activity. Perhaps by so doing, they are performing some religious service, giving the ceremonial due to traditional analyst-like activities. Certainly there is little evidence within a highly institutionalized environment that quantitative techniques lead to profit-producing results. Most studies involved in forecasting earnings per share have suggested that analysts in general have no skill at this activity; furthermore, even in those few areas where they have skill, it has not been rewarding. The only reason forecasting earnings per share must be done in an economic environment is that clients and others think it is useful, although it cannot be verified.

The technique of accounting used today was not devised for reporting to outside shareholders. It is cost accounting based upon historic figures. It compensates for its deficiencies in meeting investor reporting objectives by its accuracy: the books balance and the accounting principles, limited though they may be, are sufficiently well stated so that they can be duplicated by a variety of different accounting firms and be reasonably comparable. The trouble is that it just doesn't represent useful information for investment decision-making.

The terminology used in investor accounting can be a problem. We use concepts like "asset value" to suggest a transfer price when none is present. I can remember a mutual-fund shareholder—a minister on the West Coast—writing me and wondering why he had to pay capital gains taxes two years in a row on a capital gains distribution from his fund when the asset value had gone down. No one had apparently told him when he bought the fund at net asset value that he was picking up accrued capital gains tax liability which had been attributable to the holding period of prior investors in the fund.

Earnings per share suggest a notion of cash in the register at the end of the year that could be paid out to shareholders or reinvested aggressively in new businesses at the option of the management. Few people consciously recognize that earnings per share may include a large component of the accountant's estimate of future cash that will be received. Leasing companies take into current income part of the residual value of the estimated resale value of equipment they may sell in ten years. Insurance companies count as earnings part of the commission costs required to generate new sales contracts. These are not earnings in the sense that they are something one can spend; rather they are estimates of future cash flows, and the estimates may fall very wide of the mark.

There is little an investor can do to break these figures apart. An institutional investor could, but most have developed such a cynical attitude that they are concerned only with reported earnings per share, rather than in making any adjustment for unusual depreciation practices or adjustments to arrive at any quality of earnings index. Some attempts are being made now to arrive at a conception of discretionary cash flow, or free cash flow. This figure would adjust for higher costs of replacement equipment, the time element from which one can forecast future flows, and the discount rate at which these flows must revert to present value. None of these factors is present in the use of earnings per share. Perhaps one of the reasons why securities drop to a very low earnings multiple in an inflationary period is because the investor is intuitively responding to the notion that earnings (as a valuation technique) may not be a meaningful concept.

Current price-level accounting has been criticized by the Financial Analyst's Federation. The source of distress is that it is the function of financial analysts and not of accountants to make estimates. This view is parochial, since few financial analysts have the information (in fact, they would be prevented from having the information) required to make adjustments that the accountants make. Current price-level accounting is essential at rates of inflation in excess of 5 percent; they may be desirable under all conditions, anyway. If the information required to make the adjustments to current price level cannot be broadly disseminated, at least a company's own accountants should have that information, and accounting firms will develop good or poor reputations on their ability to arrive at correct appraisals.

Accounting is critical for investment decision-making if one is employing quantitative techniques. We will see in the future a sharp increase in use of accounting information for investment decision-making, and more accounting people are specializing in shareholder reporting with special reports for that purpose, rather than merely producing an adaptation of reports designed for companies to monitor their internal progress.

The top-down approach, as mentioned previously, starts with the economy. If, for a large institution, stock selection is not a worthwhile activity, then surely the differences in results will be made by skills in dealing with macro-issues. Questions, such as mix among cash, bonds, and stock; industry ratings; defensive positions; and so forth, will be the principal determinants of investment results.

These issues can be dealt with by experienced people only. Many economic forecasts are available from well-qualified sources through the daily newspaper, and most large investors have their own economic staff making independent gross-national-product estimates. In fact, most businessmen consider themselves good amateur economists and have some views as to whether the economy is likely to move up or down. A smaller number of people will be able to derive independently a forecast for the national-income accounts but will have some impressions which amount to the same result.

An independent economic forecast, however, is not useful in the investment area if it merely confirms the consensus. The fact that a consensus exists suggests that it has already been discounted by market action and to act on the consensus is not rewarding. The practice I subscribe to is the identification of the economic consensus and an examination of those parts of the consensus with which I might disagree. Within this conflict are many profitable opportunities for investment.

The conventional forecast recently was that inflation rates would decline as business plateaued in 1973–1974. The bond market was priced to suggest that inflation rates would be imbedded at 5 percent or 6 percent, which was the conventional forecast of inflation rates by institutional investors. They ignored the fact that overseas rates were considerably higher and rising. Furthermore, inflationary expectations were built into union contracts and consumers' behavior was likely to push prices above the 10 percent level. In a structured, controlled economy, free market forces, like mild recessions, do not bring prices down except in the very late stages.

An inflationary forecast was a nonconsensus position. It identified the investment opportunities in commodity-oriented industries and other fields, like chemicals, operating at capacity where prices could be promptly raised to reflect new conditions. Coincidentally, these fields were also quite asset rich, providing them with other desirable characteristics within a classic inflationary environment.

Few economists take pride in their recent forecasting ability. Most use government figures which have contained a number of statistical and sampling errors. Also, they are, for the most part, domestically oriented with very little experience in international monetary conditions, the Euro-dollar market, and business cycles abroad. Few economists specialize in the relationship between economies, yet many are experts on a single economy. As the world moves toward greater independence through the adoption of increased international trade, the traditional economic tools will be found wanting.

Economists have been befuddled by the American economy since 1971 when price controls were established. We have gone through the first American inflationary recession. This type of recession is without precedent in the post-World War II United States, but it is quite like the economic pauses which characterized the European recovery. It may well be that the United States has adopted the full characteristics of the Atlantic Alliance membership.

Few economists recognize the parallels between the United States and Europe: socially, economically, and politically. In prior years the United States worker was striving to achieve mobility for his family, to obtain a college education, and thereby graduate from blue-collar to white-collar ranks. A college education is now available in the United States to nearly anyone with minimal skills. Work effort by a blue-collar worker is not a prerequisite for the next generation to make this transition. On the contrary, it appears socially desirable for many white-collar children to join trades and work with their hands. Blue-collar work has been upgraded, financially and socially, to such an extent that it is no longer a status or financial barrier.

Family incomes have risen by the pattern of women working. A wife may work for domestic independence rather than for economic necessity. Our currency is no longer the bulwark of Western trade now that we have exported dollars to the world in return for consumer goods. Our currency is subject to the same pressures and fluctuations of any other major country, but it remains immune to pressure from none. Politically, we will probably enter a phase of strong legislative government, a characteristic of our European partners.

The American businessman even looks like his European counterpart more each day. He has had a full order book for some time, and yet he is pessimistic about the future. He has liquidity strains from borrowed capital and is facing inflation rates that have only been seen in Europe, Japan, and the more stable countries of South America. He, too, is behaving like his European counterpart. American consumers, in the face of uncertainty are taking down consumer debt and buying durable goods before they become unavailable at present prices.

One of the principal roles economists can play in the investment process is that of a high-level tipster. To the extent that economists are called in as consultants in government and industry, they pass on the insights received from these different activities to investment institutions. I can think of no case where economists violated a specific confidence. But I can think of many where economists were useful in conveying impressions they received from visits with government officials in Washington.

Nearly all the leading economists who have dealt with the investment community have been active consultants to our government. Many have been members of the Council of Economic Advisors. When I was director of research for F. S. Moseley & Co., one member of the Council was my brokerage client while he was in Washington. Every six months, I would receive a telephone call from Washington with the same conversation. He would ask how I felt about different sectors of the economy, the market, interest rates, and overseas conditions. Each time I started to give an answer, he would cut me off in the middle. I had the feeling that once I began my answer, the economist knew what it would be. This continued to the benefit of my commission business for several years. All the time I felt that I was perhaps having some hand in shaping the economic recommendations that were going to the President.

I was dismayed, however, to think that my forecasts might have been worthwhile, based upon the sketchy information that was available to me at that time. My experience with economists as investors tends to place them into two camps—either wildly speculative, as they treat the stock market as a nonserious number game, or excessively conservative. Like many academics, they tend toward the gloomy side and are not very anxious to risk even a small amount of capital. Rarely, and in no case to my knowledge, are their own investment programs well balanced.

All of the leading economists who deal with investment people are articulate and scholarly. This combination would be rare in most other fields, but I suspect that articulateness is essential in order to convert their research work into a marketable product for investors.

Another influence in determining the value of a company may be its name. Some companies have an old, moss-covered title like Pacific Car & Foundry which may no longer be appropriate for the business in which the company is pre-eminent. Pacific Car & Foundry has the largest single share of truck manufacturing business west of the Mississippi—an outgrowth of its original business, the manufacture of railroad cars. It correctly changed with the times and saw itself in the manufacturing business for transportation units, rather than merely suffering from the marketing myopia of providing railroad cars to a no-growth industry. The company recently changed its name to PACCAR—a name which ties in with its past but gives no specific hint of what type of transportation business is being transacted.

The name changes which took place in the late sixties have been well documented. The addition of "onics" and "natics" gave the impression of far more technological content to many companies than was supported by the facts. Companies which had small divisions in exotic areas assumed the name of the smaller division and ignored the more prosaic, basic part of the business which was associated with low multiples.

Often, by the time the name changes became effective, the change was motivated by factors which had long since ceased to be influential. Some companies with small health units, for example, would adopt a name suggesting they were dominant in the health-care industry, yet that industry might have ceased to become a recognized glamour field. Name changes to influence stock valuation by association with a recognized glamour field are very likely to be unproductive. It is an indication to investors that caution in that field should be observed.

Another type of name change which may confuse investors centers around companies which have gotten into trouble and have frequently split themselves apart, changing their name in order that an unpleasant history be left behind. Saturn Industries was one of the hot glamour issues of the sixties which collapsed late in the decade. The three divisions which had been consistently profitable were kept, reformed, and named Tyler Corporation. A growth track of those three divisions remained consistent through the sixties. Therefore, Tyler was unblemished by the decline of its larger predecessor, Saturn.

Name changes often involve a reconstruction of past

records. The most innovative reconstruction and name change to my knowledge was the creation of Computer Technology Corporation by James Ling in the mid sixties. While Ling was engaged in "Operation Redeployment"— selling off small pieces of his subsidiary companies to the public in order to establish separate public markets for each division—he concluded correctly that it would be wise to have a high multiple, computer-related activity within his complex.

The only part of LTV that was doing much with computing was his own tabulating department, preparing invoices and doing regular mundane accounting chores. How could one glamorize such an inherently unglamorous field? With the bravado for which he became justly famous, Ling decided to spin off his accounting department, recreate a record from cost-accounting figures of what the payroll and absorption of overhead would have been for that department, name it Computer Technology, and hire a top-notch IBM salesman as president with instructions to get additional business.

Computer Technology was created and spun off, and it achieved a high market valuation. Several years after it had a separate identity, Ling sold the company for a huge profit. Prudential Insurance bought the parent company's interest in Computer Technology for about $20 million. After the sale, Ling was said to have been amazed at being able to take a staff function, such as accounting, and sell it to a sophisticated investor at a huge premium.

Name changes often involve related accounting modifications. Accountants allow numbers to be discarded if they relate to noncontinuing operations. A parent company can then wipe out past losses by erasing them in the present. The sale or, for that matter, just the planned sale of an existing activity is enough to allow an auditor to go back and expunge the contribution of a mistake in the prior years.

Fuqua Industries, which has not changed its name for some years, is a company that seems to be increasing its earnings by 20 percent annually to the $2.50 level. Each year, it reports earnings in the $2.50 per share area, which are up from a restated figure of $2.00 for the prior year. The explanation is always a reduction in the contribution of subsidiaries that are to be discontinued.

In selecting a security, one should be aware of event investing. Brokers like to promote securities that involve a specific reason for the security to be bought immediately. One of the greatest problems they have is in interesting a potential client in taking action on a security that same day.

The broker can tell his client: "XYZ must be bought today because event W will happen next week, which will make the stock go up." Occasionally, significant events can be forecast in advance, but this occurs so rarely that it is not worth the effort to be sensitive to events of that nature. Inside information, as we know, is illegal. An investor in possession of information which might influence a significant price change is legally prohibited from acting upon such information.

From time to time, it is possible to act upon information that is already in the public domain but has not been disseminated. Some information, although significant, may be well ahead of price changes. Securities that are owned by individuals are frequently not as responsive to information in such publications as *The Wall Street Journal* as those owned by institutions. After all, individual investors do not have access to the same sources as the institutions and anyone reading these conventional sources has a simple proprietary advantage. Even items like dividend increases, historically closely correlated with price changes, are not fully discounted by individual investors until the higher dividend

check is received. That is the only time at which some individual shareholders know that a dividend increase has taken
place, even though the amount of the dividend is automati-
cally deducted from the market price of the stock on the day
it sells "ex-dividend."

In 1969, the Food and Drug Administration banned
the use of cyclamates in soft drinks. Studies had shown that
large quantities of cyclamate would cause death in rats and,
therefore, by government fiat the rapidly growing diet-drink
industry was wiped out. To my knowledge, there was no advance warning of this development, and it had great implications. Clearly, the bottlers would not slow down but
would attempt to sell their diet-branded drinks with some
amount of sugar.

Sugar is a commodity where small changes in volume,
one could argue, influence a large change in price. Sugar
stocks on the morning of the announcement had a delayed
opening and rose 25 percent from their previous night's
close. The event was a specific action by government, the
projected result would be a forecasted increase in sugar
sales, with higher prices and substantially larger profits for
the sugar companies.

The sugar stocks were selling at low multiples and
high yields anyway at this time, so this news incrementally
should have been very attractive to them. However, there
were many other reasons for the unattractiveness of sugar
stocks. Principal among them was the fact that the market
was undergoing a large decline, concentrated in low-quality
isues.

I discussed the implications of the government
change with a group of brokerage salesmen that morning
and suggested that they recommend sugar stocks to their
customers. They were eager for this story, and I was anxious
to give them something to sell. It was a classic event situation. Unfortunately, it also had the classic result: once the

event wore off—in this case within about a day—underlying factors took hold and no one made any money on the recommendation. Events tend to momentarily distract investors from the underlying principles affecting stock prices, but they are hardly ever durable. Purchases or sales made on a short war, a presidential assassination, or the like, are more like to succeed by betting against the event than for it.

4
Portfolio Construction

I can remember my first opportunity to have discretionary control over large sums of institutional money. In the mid sixties, there was a period that became known as the "superstar days." Rapid-fire, off-the-cuff decision-making was its main characteristic. Committees were frowned upon, and portfolio managers were charged with the responsibility of moving funds quickly and aggressively into securities where there was the greatest immediate profit potential.

One reason for this structure was that there always would be someone on an investment committee who remembered an unpleasant experience in some industry that might under present-day conditions offer profit. The best way to circumvent this impediment in the late stages of a bull market was "to rent a kid"; that is, hire someone who had no preconceptions about particular investment alternatives.

It was in this setting that I assumed management of over $300 million of aggressive funds. I had an almost complete mandate to do whatever was necessary to achieve the desired result—to attain and maintain a position at the top of the list of competitive growth funds.

The new manager tends to concentrate quite heavily in what may have been the consensus before he assumed responsibility for the portfolio. In my own case, I have rarely felt that the institutional consensus in investment management is rewarding (consensus may often be right, but often it has been fully discounted in prices). I was attracted to unusually large positions in heavily institutionalized, low-multiple securities; the securities whose earnings had gone up much faster than price and those cyclical stocks not necessarily tied directly to the business cycle.

The largest position I instituted was in the airlines, approximately 17 percent of the total portfolio. Airlines are very volatile securities: not all of them fly in "friendly skies." They move in and out of institutional favor on wide swings in earnings. I was biased in favor of the group anyway as I had done some pioneering research on airline securities several years earlier. It was theoretically possible to forecast their earnings, hence their price, on the basis of equipment purchases. In the late sixties, however, equipment purchases slowed down and the principal issue was guessing at traffic growth. In this industry small increments in traffic produce large earnings gains. At this time the projection of traffic on its past trend of growth of twice the rate of the economy would have produced earnings gains in excess of 30 percent. For slightly different reasons, I also undertook excessively large nonconsensus positions in autos and aerospace. They each had a different reason for earnings gains but were also selling at an earnings multiple well below the market.

These groups were diversified according to economic forces but were undiversified relative to the market. In the bear down-trend of 1969–1970, each of these three groups substantially underperformed the market, producing painful results for any investor who was heavily committed.

Diversification

Diversification is a technique for minimizing the risks that accompany any securities venture. If a portfolio manager could look ahead and pinpoint the precise timing of a single event, he would naturally follow the right course. But since this is virtually impossible to do, he seeks to minimize the ever-present possibility of error by hedging his position through diversification. Diversification precludes putting all your investment eggs in "one basket." It should be pointed out, however, that too much diversification is worse than none at all. Just as a general of the army may invite defeat by spreading his available forces too thin, so may a portfolio manager become susceptible to error by overdiversifying the number of securities in an account.

Diversification is a frequently elusive factor for which academia has coined a new term. The investor should attempt to minimize the covariance (like the common forces on each security) among securities in his portfolio. Industry diversification isn't enough; quality diversification is not helpful. In fact, the investor may have to rely upon the historical relationships between securites and assume that such relationships, or covariants, will remain in force.

One of the better forms of diversification may be geographic. A number of interesting studies suggest that diversification in different stock markets is useful and that there is a very low correlation or covariance among foreign markets. This work suggests that portfolios in the future will be highly internationalized and will achieve better diversification without reducing returns by cutting across national borders.

In the future, most investment portfolios in the United States will be internationalized. In many respects they already are, through the activities of large American corporations. Export trade and overseas earnings are approximately a third of most large U.S. companies. They happen to be the most profitable part of their activities, although that may be due to the method by which internal accounts are kept.

Traditionally, Americans have concentrated their portfolios away from the various international capital markets. This tendency will change. Now that the U.S. currency and the economy are more closely aligned with those of the Western world, we can expect that capital will be allocated around the world and portfolios will be balanced in different currency areas.

American portfolio managers have not been good international investors. They have not understood the currency problems and have not been aware of the government forces in each of the countries where they might invest. These forces are more important than in our own country in determining investment returns. We have always expected that funds placed overseas would be returned for ultimate reinvestment. A balancing of different stock markets provides diversification that may be difficult to achieve in any one area. Our portfolios will increasingly assume the aspects of European portfolios as they were constructed ten years ago. Trips through the banking fraternities in overseas countries are good preparation for the next decade.

I know of one around-the-world trip, conducted in ten days by a brokerage firm, designed to circumnavigate the globe with briefings held at the airports of major world capitals. Unfortunately, it was a far better study of first-class international air travel than of economic conditions in the countries involved.

Americans have taken a chauvinistic attitude toward investment markets other than their own. Now that we recognize that our problems are at least as great as those of the rest of the world, the America-first policy applied to portfolios should not remain a great barrier. In fact, just as American portfolios may place some of their capital outside this country, the investments in dollars held outside the U.S. by the Europeans, Japanese, and Arabs may well be converted to longer-term investment in the United States, thus balancing the dollar outflow from American institutional portfolios.

Another form of diversification is by investment type. There are three alternatives for most publicly traded portfolios: cash, fixed income, and equity. Markets for warrants, options, convertibles, venture capital, and so forth are either amply specialized or sufficiently narrow and are understood by investors for whom such possibilities are available.

Cash has emerged as a principal diversification tool. It formerly was used as a market hedge, in conjunction with forecasts of declining prices. But its application was limited, because the returns on cash or its equivalent, principally Treasury bills or Certificates of Deposit, were usually less than the long-term rising trend rate of common stock prices. In 1974, however, cash returns were on the order of 10 percent. At the same time a major bear market was in process. Thus, cash as a diversification tool seems to carry a lower price tag, particularly if an investor cannot conveniently dampen the volatility of a portfolio due to the instability of short-term equity risks. Cash may be the only way in which a portfolio can be conveniently dampened. Fixed-income alternatives, principally bonds, used to be the main offset to equities in a typically balanced portfolio. In fact, as bonds appreciated, equities declined and vice versa.

A number of market timing systems were developed in conjunction with the opposite moving forces between bonds and equities. Essentially, lower interest rates would be associated with a reduced demand for funds in a recessionary condition, or the government's stimulus of business, by making money easier. Under such circumstances, bonds would appreciate in price while equities declined, reflecting more difficult business conditions or reduced earnings, accompanied by dividend cuts or omissions.

Historical studies have suggested that the true rate of return on bonds, adjusted for inflation, was something on the order of 3 to 3½ percent (some have computed figures as low as 1 percent), and that the actual rate might be more nearly the real rate, plus the rate of imbedded inflation. It could be assumed, in a period of declining business, that bond rates could come down, because of a slight adjustment in the expected real rate of return, perhaps from 3½ to 2½ percent, and that prices would moderate, reflecting the newer competitive environment of both labor and goods under recession conditions. Declining interest rates would raise bond prices, producing better results for the balanced portfolio which had a substantial portion of fixed-income obligations.

Diversification through fixed income became quite expensive during the twenty-five-year bull market which ended in 1966, especially if one of the market cycles was missed. It became increasingly apparent that long-term oriented funds, like pension and endowment funds, should have a much higher proportion of equities and not attempt to call a market turn. Failure caused by missing a cycle would produce an opportunity loss of 20 to 30 percent. This would seriously penalize the long-term result. Diversification turned out to be too expensive to utilize for a typical portfolio, which might have had bonds during the latter part of the sixties with low interest rates and high expectations for equity prices.

A recent diversification technique being used by institutional investors is to split fund managements. Ten years ago accounts were split to create a competitive position. It was assumed that managers would respond in line with their own commercial interests for competitive accounts. A large fund might be split into several parts and entrusted to several managers. Operating costs were higher, since most of the managers had progressively lower charges on the incrementally higher dollars. Motivation was expected to offset this operational limitation.

One of the principal purposes investment management clients have in splitting a fund apart is to obtain information on different investment styles. The problem of performance measurement is to determine the time over which it is relevant. Not only do performance measurements, like stock classifications, have to be adjusted for volatility levels, but one has to determine whether there is a minimum amount of time in which it is relevant, or is it indeed, as some say, one full market cycle.

Furthermore, is every market cycle like every other market cycle, so that perhaps one market cycle alone is not enough? There is a tendency to use performance measurements over far too short a period of time and even one full market cycle may be too short.

Recently diversification has been following more specialized paths. The equity man of the sixties was expected to be the Renaissance Man. He supposedly was able to operate in bonds, stocks, and in different types of market environments—"the compleat investor." Now it is assumed that the best investor is the narrow, specialized, and disciplined individual who has his own operating trademark. Perhaps at all times, even when a particular style is out of favor, investors will be able to differentiate between them and pick the principal proponent from each style category. It is assumed, then, that each will rotate eventually into favor at some point in the market cycle. This is known as diversification within equity styles. It may involve income stocks, venture capital, special situations, and even institutional consensus investing.

The emerging trend in the quest for diversification

without penalizing results is the stress on mechanical strategies. Increasingly, no investor has a proprietary information
edge over other investors. In fact, there are substantial legal
prohibitions that suggest that buyer and seller must together
have identical information about the security they propose
to deal in. They may differ in judgment, but even that is
rather difficult if they were similarly trained and similarly
motivated and receive the information at approximately the
same time. Accepting a notion of this perfect information
world leads investors to operate with a series of mechanical
rules. A set of rules allows him to operate against a pricing inefficiency that may exist for a very short time, so that he
does not have to spend the conventional time of making an
economic analysis or an on-the-spot judgment as to the motivation of management and its future plans.

Quantifiable rules (sometimes called "screens") provide for the operation of portfolios containing larger numbers of securities than have been true in the past. These
rules achieve more controlled diversification and a better examination of the causal factors that produce results. Mechanical strategies suit the age of computers in investment
decision-making and perhaps could only have evolved
through the frustration of dealing with more conventional
techniques.

I am quite convinced that, while many investors
think they are adopting the conventional techniques of economic and corporate analysis, they really are employing a
limited number of quantifiable rules that worked in the
most recent market period. The intelligent investor would
tend to downgrade these rules from the most recent market
period, since that is probably the condition most firmly
planted in an investor's mind and discounted in the
marketplace.

Diversification can be achieved without lowering performance. It may be a tool to achieve higher performance,

adjusting for uncertainty, and may become adjunctive to the use of mechanical strategies when constructing portfolios over the next decade.

Security classification systems have received a continuous amount of attention. At Keystone Funds in Boston at least one person is kept busy working out new classification schemes, with which to compare the various elements of a portfolio against acceptable targets.

A classification system is designed to provide information about the way a portfolio is balanced. The normal portfolio breakdown and balance is directed more towards sources of net income than towards schemes that relate the holdings to industries or to economic effects like business cycles. If a portfolio is designed to be responsive to market forces, then the quantitative terms that relate to its breakdown and volatility characteristics should be most predictive of expectations under a predetermined set of future circumstances.

Portfolio breakdown techniques are often used in connection with different performance measures. Brokers in bull markets publicize an unweighted index of the market results derived from their research recommendations. Rarely do they publish such figures in a bear market. Mutual funds keep close track of how the competition is doing and whether they stand above or below average. Most mutual-fund organizations attempt to spread their funds sufficiently so that they will have at least one entrant in the upper categories irrespective of general market conditions. Most investment managers submit their performance data to measurement services like Becker Securities and Frank Russell & Co., so that they can use performance figures to support their case if they are favorable or ignore them if they are unfavorable.

Some investors use regular indices, like Standard & Poor's industry breakdowns. Others devise their own in terms like defensive, cyclical, or growth. Still others use quantitative measures, such as separating securities according to volatility characteristics or price objectives under certain market hypotheses. Whichever classification is used, the investor must weigh the advantages and disadvantages of each.

The one very strong advantage of using a market index, such as provided by Standard & Poor's or Dow Jones, for performance measurements is that their investment selections are available at low cost. For most investors they most nearly approximate a randomization of the market and can readily be duplicated with some sampling techniques. Once one elects to duplicate a market index, the proprietary work of the firm elected would be to minimize client expenses.

Expense control would insure a closer relationship between theoretical returns and actual returns than might otherwise be the case. What has been called index-matching is really the first of a series of mechanical strategies. Index-matching, which has substantial advantages for very large portfolios, is like stripping the investment business of its mystique and recognizing that the emperor is walking down the street naked.

Index-matching offers consistency by definition, since it will closely approximate the performance measure established for it by the market index. It is economical since most costs can be predetermined. It should, over a time, compare favorably for most large funds against an actively managed account. More directly, it will encourage managers who have specialized skills to engage in those skills other than merely duplicating the work that can be done by mechanical strategy. It will return the artists to his art, rather than have him spend his time on making frames.

A number of portfolios have been strikingly similar to an index portfolio without admitting it. The large mutual fund, Massachusetts Investors Trust (MIT), has a volatility of approximately 1.0 and nearly a zero alpha, suggesting that the fund approximates the market. There is every reason why it should. It is so large it virtually has to be at market risk at all times, but one can easily raise the question, why a large staff of portfolio managers and analysts are required to duplicate this task. One could borrow from the collective judgment and wisdom of the investment community by accepting the notion that the securities in which it must deal are efficiently priced.

If MIT's objective is to do as well as the market, minus its expenses, which are lower than many funds, then it comes very close to meeting those objectives. It is an example of a modest objective with an investment strategy designed to have a high probability of meeting that objective. Since satisfactions of this nature are unique within the investment community, index-matching may be merely an extension of existing practice, rather than a new revolution.

Identifying Market Phases

Next to diversification techniques, the nearly impossible task of identifying the nature of market forces is critical in portfolio construction. The error rate will be high but not nearly high enough to make the effort worthless. I doubt if any investor can afford to disregard this second key consideration, especially at major turning points.

Many investors can do this systematically, but the present consensus is that one should not even try. Investors may take the attitude that they will participate in all markets or none at all, or they will attempt to find a system that suits almost all conditions. Unfortunately, the worst thing that one can do in a poor market is to employ technical tools that are designed for good markets. Relative strength, for example, is perhaps one of the more compellingly poor guides to use in a bear market. Many investors, particularly institutions, tend in a bad market to sell securities that have been behaving the worst and buy those that have been the best performers. This is a distinctly awkward tactic that oftentimes causes one to switch into a security that is on the verge of a new decline. The same tactic may be another expression of the commonly followed activity that involves moving up the quality scale as the market decline continues.

Most bad markets cascade, with the lowest quality issues dropping first. Sometimes this is reflected by the American Stock Exchange price index declining before the New York Stock Exchange Composite Index. Low-quality securities seem especially depressed relative to earnings at the peak of the market, whereas their earnings are probably increasing at a greater rate than the top-grade securities. They generally rank second or third in an industry, but have a greater rate of increase in new sales. The operating leverage for such companies may be slightly higher than for the companies of better quality.

Nearly everything imaginable tends to force one into poor quality companies at, or just after, a bull market tops out and the move in a southerly direction begins. To be loaded up with low-quality securities at the start of a bear market and to upgrade gradually as the decline progresses is one of the surest ways to invite a burial by subscription later on.

The correct method, assuming that one is not going to employ cash, is to shift the low-quality securities gradually to higher quality, and the more volatile to more defensive securities as the market progresses upward. As the market recedes, the quality of the securities can be gradually lowered until the lowest quality is achieved at what might be a bottom level.

There is virtually no way to pinpoint an exact market bottom, of which there are classical types. One is the emotional, high-volume release usually associated with climactic events. Under these circumstances, prices behave completely irrationally. Securities are sold regardless of price into thin and unreceptive markets. Margin calls are common. Purchases made under these forced conditions have a high probability of success.

The other type of classical bottom is called an "exhaustion" bottom. Here the market just gets tired from going down. There are neither buyers nor sellers at these low prices that are often not associated with any specific event. These two bottom characteristics are the most common, but not necessarily the only conditions under which a market turn may be made. I suspect that market valuations, like individual securities, are nearly always an intelligent assessment of current conditions. It may be only during occasional extreme circumstances that inefficiency sneaks in and only for short periods of less than a year. The half-life principle seems as appropriate for the general markets as for individual stocks.

We had a recent opportunity to observe an important market cycle reverse. I visited the financial district in New York on May 25, 1970—one day before the panic low of 628 on the Dow Industrials. At that time, the corner of Broad and Wall was guarded by 500 mounted police. Their function was unrelated to the financial community; there were riots between construction workers and pedestrians. But I came away with a sense of chagrin at seeing the nation's financial center under police guard.

I felt this was a close approximation to the Rothschild dictum about "buying 'rentes' when there was blood in the streets." As it happened, 1970 was also the year of the Kent State incident, in which national guard troops fired on rioting students. One could not pinpoint a reason to be bullish for a single event, but there were several emotional signals that usually characterize in important trend reversal.

In this particular case, there was also the convenience

of large volume*—a further classical sign of a major market bottom. The market declined again and successfully tested its May 26 low in June on sharply reduced volume. This further confirmed the classical definition of a major turnaround.

My firm, Batterymarch, at that time was investing in high-quality, high-yield industries. We had especially large positions in oil and tobacco stocks. Our reason for holding them was not that they would produce maximum gain. Like others, we were mainly trying to find ways to hedge our investments in the event that the market continued to go down, in which case we would want to be in less volatile securities. These industries became market leaders of the late 1970 period. We were able to take quick profits and reinvest the proceeds in a more dynamic selection of companies—principally life, fire, and casualty insurance and banks.

In a normal sense, an investment in high-yield securities at the bottom would have represented rather neutral strategy. It just happened that this particular market did not behave in an entirely normal manner on the recovery. But it did lead us to conclude that high-yielding, relatively stable securities are quite likely to perform better than their more volatile counterparts in the early phase of a market rise. Investors may want to reduce their cash position and participate in a market turn, but they are not wholly confident about the situation. Therefore, they pick these hedged securities, which was our practice as well.

There is a tendency in a rising market to become price unconscious, to let one's gains move on further than

---

* N.Y.S.E. volume in May 1970 totaled 258,220,000 shares—averaging about 12.3 million shares daily in twenty-one trading sessions. The turnover in June averaged 10.3 million and 10.4 million in July. August was low volume month for the year with 218.7 million shares traded.

one thinks is reasonable and to buy quite aggressively before prices move out of sight. In the early stages of a bull market this is quite a satisfactory procedure. However, in the late stages, one runs a high risk of being swept along with the crowd. It is very difficult, with foresight, to identify the various stages of market development.

The classical form has changed many times, and just as greed tends to overtake rational behavior at market tops and fear sets in at the bottom, most investors adjust for the market condition that has just passed. It is my view that that is the one condition, because of this technique of discounting prices, which can be ignored.

It is difficult to imagine that anyone could not invest successfully during a bull market. The trouble is that some people credit their own brilliance to a stock's ability to appreciate in price, and this makes them overconfident. They should realize that bull markets have their pitfalls, as do bear markets. Bull markets are but a prelude to the next inevitable declining phase, and investors' switch over from a bearish to a bullish psychology should be accomplished gracefully and with the utmost care. There is never anything "easy" about the market, irrespective of the prevailing trend.

It seems natural now to pinpoint the May 1970 low as a clear signal of a market reversal but it was difficult at the time. Volume was high and prices fell emotionally for almost four weeks. Except for certain periods in 1973–1974, it was the longest panic decline since I entered the investment business. After the first week of heavy selling, it seemed clear to me that reversal was imminent, although the precise price level and timing were impossible to forecast. The main thing was that the decline that had started the previous year was over. The reservoirs of cash that remained uncommitted on the market sidelines should be reinvested immediately. But in what?

Volatile stocks are the most profitable to own in the very low foothills of a new bull market. Keystone Funds has a unique separation of fully invested equity funds in which the manager cannot build up cash positions and is, therefore, ready at the bottom in a fully invested portfolio of a defined quality type. The Keystone system, devised by a noninvestment man in the thirties, separates the common-stock universe into four groups—the so-called S-1 through S-4. Each higher grade is roughly more volatile, or riskier, than the grade that precedes it. The most famous fund, S-4, is a selection of highly speculative sccurites which, although very painful to own in a declining market, responds very quickly during the early stages of a rise.

These funds provide many useful clues for determining the character of a market because the managers can affect only the selection of stocks and not the quality of the portfolio. Internally, Keystone has an excellent tool called the "contominant variable," a ratio of actual results against the results of a universe from which the manager can pick his stocks. This index is far more than a comparison with a market index; it keeps the organization up to date on the manager's activities. There have been notable occasions when the character of the market favored one particular style of investing, such as one Keystone fund or another when the selectivity was down ("poor CV"), but was considered to be an excellent performance by the investment fraternity.

Although the usual type of gain from the bottom is in volatile securities, other types may do better, or at least better than might be expected. If yield is most desirable, high-income stocks might be the leaders, especially if they have other characteristics such as a low dividend payout with high probability of an increase. In the fifties asset-rich stocks were the leaders. It is far more important to identify individual stocks that are likely to pace the market upward than to know the industry to which they belong. Ideally, the single security most likely to show the greatest profit is one on the brink of bankruptcy when the market first begins to turn. With high leverage—assuming it is reorganized in time—it soon regains financial health and prosperity. No investor, to my knowledge, has the skill to accurately time such an event. If he happens to do so, such good fortune should be ascribed more to luck than to his own financial acumen.

Impartiality

The probabilities considered in portfolio optimization and game theory are used to determine a future course of action. The outcome of these decisions determines whether the result will bring rewards or penalties. The portfolio manager usually focuses attention on the one most likely outcome. He has a single favorite security, or industry, or market hypothesis, and one economic forecast. His tendency is to incorporate this set of outcomes into his investment thinking and to exclude all else from mind.

A good example of this procedure is that for many years there has been some possibility, however remote, of a worldwide depression and economic holocaust. Few investment managers consciously consider this very seriously. They are concerned that by doing so they would adopt such a dismal frame of mind that they would be unable to operate at all. However, when such a long-odds forecast becomes more probable, it looms as an enormous surprise and causes the portfolio manager, who should have been continually adjusting his portfolio for this small but perhaps increasing possibility, to be shocked and dismayed.

The place one goes to reach major portfolio construction decisions is especially important. Few good investment decisions are reached in the office due to the bias of former thought patterns. In mid-1968 the market was recovering in the expectation that we would move into a very exciting period in the seventies. We called them "The Soaring Seventies."

Considering that we had a very speculative market in 1967, investment opinions returned quickly to the idea that prosperous conditions were returning. I was running a $350 million growth fund at the time and was troubled by this universal acceptance of optimism. Finding that everyone held the same idea, I initiated a practice that I have followed many times since.

I left the office for several days to go away by myself to think. I sought people who were not directly involved in the day-to-day investment business. At that time, I went to New York to talk to businessmen, bankers, and just a few investment people. I returned to Boston convinced that investment managers were attempting to project their own optimism upon an already inflated market.

I wrote a memo and circulated it throughout the organization, itemizing in points 1 through 8 my concern about the investment outlook and the economy. These thoughts were diametrically opposed to our own investment policy and the views of our economic department. An economist was assigned to provide a critique of my memo, which he did by expounding a strong positive case for the consensus.

Knowing that my fund was expected to be an appreciation fund, I decided to buy low-multiple, nonconsensus industries as protection against what I saw coming for the market rather than assuming a cash position. This hedged position helped somewhat in the first stage of the decline. After six months, however, I began looking for signs that the decline was over. Now others in the organization began to feel that the decline would continue perpetually, if only because the trend was well established. For my part, I knew that market declines had rarely lasted more than nine months since World War II, and that my fund, having taken a defensive position initially, should become more aggressive. My technique in doing so was to increase the weighting in those defensive areas of low-multiple issues that had held up so well.

There are several lessons to be learned from this procedure. 1) In the middle of a bear market, buying industries that have performed best is a poor idea. They are more likely to catch up with the overall market on the downside than they are to continue to be resistive. 2) Low multiples of earnings are rarely good protection in the early or middle stages of a market decline. 3) Attempting to time a market decline purely on duration in relationship to past historic norms is likely to be faulty. This market decline endured from the middle of 1968 until May 1970. When it turned, it turned quite suddenly.

5

Investment Motives

There is something backward about who invests in what and why. Individual investors often are taxed at high rates, yet they frequently invest for yield. In most such portfolios I have seen, there is a reasonably high taxable income level. Tax-free institutions tend to invest for appreciation, which has a tax-sheltered capital gains feature. The theoretical notion is that a company's retained earnings are reinvested directly in the company and thus plowed back into the nation's corporate enterprises rather than distributed as dividends upon which taxes are paid.

Individuals should invest in the type of companies in which institutions predominate and vice versa. A change may be taking place today in that there is increasing interest by institutions in the current income part of the total return equation. That may be one explanation for the better-than-expected performance of yield stocks in 1973–1974.

The individual investor is the ultimate beneficiary of all the efforts of the investment process. He may act independently, deciding to forego consumption in order to have investment capital. He may, on the other hand, be an involuntary investor through required pension and profit-sharing plans. He may financially support the local hospital or church, which may be an investor. If that fund fares well with its investment, the requirement for his support may be diminished. It is difficult to imagine any person so far removed from the private capital system that he is not directly affected by the investment process.

The typical individual acting for himself may make his own investment decisions through a broker or a bank. He may also delegate a part or all of the decision responsibility to professionals—insurance companies, mutual funds, or investment managers. Whether he is selecting particular securities for himself or choosing someone to act for him, he is going far down the line with the process. This discussion is intended to illuminate some of the issues involved in the steps that must be taken.

The individual investor has a good intuitive sense about what to do. While he does not run detailed performance studies, he knows if he buys something and it goes up in price, he has a profit and does not need to compare this result with what might have happened to the general market.

The individual investor frequently invests for fun. He prefers to buy stocks in industries that he understands. For example, if he has a special knowledge of the retailing industry, it is added pleasure to follow retailing more closely through reading stock reports and such. He is responsive to dividend increases and feels, quite correctly, that this is a sign of the financial health of the companies he owns.

The typical investor becomes involved with what he reads about the managements of his companies and identifies with them. This is an opportunity that the managements of companies rarely exploit. Managements often try to court the institutional investor and meet him personally, but they hardly ever engage in a financial public-relations campaign designed to personify company managements for individual investors.

The individual investor frequently encourages his children to own a few shares of stock—as one gives an allowance to a child—and to follow them closely. The children thus learn how to cultivate capital. Few companies have exploited this common educational function of investors.

The individual investor necessarily relies quite heavily upon his broker. Unfortunately, many individuals feel that the broker does not place his customers' interests first. In the late sixties the observation, "Where are the Customers' Yachts?"* applied particularly to clients who were sold hot issues that proceeded to go down and never recover.

Individuals tend to buy less volatile stocks than institutions yet they are not as impressed by well-known names. Rather, they are influenced by their own personal familiarity with what the company does. There are very few individuals today, for example, who would buy the low-yielding, high-multiple drug group. The product lines are not readily identifiable to the individual, the industry is complex, and the securities are selling at expensive prices.

---

* An observation credited to William R. Travers, celebrated stutterer and wit and a member of the New York Stock Exchange in the post-Civil War period. Travers resided in Newport in the summer, where he kept a small-sized yacht, which he obtained in lieu of a debt. While watching a yacht race one afternoon from the deck of his craft, he noticed a boat coming alongside in which was a committee that had been assigned to pay him the respects of the squadron. He noticed that they nearly all happened to be bankers or brokers. Casting his eyes across the water to some beautiful white-winged yachts, Travers found by inquiry that they all belonged to Wall Street brokers. With his gaze still resting on the handsome squadron, he asked his distinguished visitors: "But wh-wh-where are the cu-cu-customers' yachts?"

The principal objective of most investors is to make as much money as possible without losing any. I have seen four pages of detailed objectives from sophisticated investors, which not only lay down broad targets under different types of market conditions but also present quite definitive operating rules of what to do if a loss occurs, what to do if there is a gain, and so on.

I am personally attracted to the notion of a mobile objective; that is, the reestablishment of investment objectives as market conditions change and are perceived. In a falling market, preparing for the next rise becomes paramount. Contrariwise, if one is in a market rise, one should begin to focus on the reverse side of that condition.

The point of a specific percentage objective expressed as some return over a time, is quite often useful in hindsight and may develop a familiarity between investment manager and client but does little to alter the behavior of the investment manager in dealing with his clients.

Unless one is investing venture capital, I agree with the notion that one cannot expect to become rich by investing in the public market without a considerable amount of luck. For those who have the responsibility to invest, the best thing to do is maintain purchasing power. It is probably more important to study results in the light of changes in purchasing power rather than as is traditionally done in comparisons with a market average or with the results achieved by competitors.

The written objectives of some investors are illuminating. They usually charge the investment manager to "do as well as you can without losing anything," accompanied by a hopeful pat on the back. Some are stated more succinctly in "legalese":

> We understand that the investment objective of the Account is total return, taking into account both appreciation and yield, at an acceptable level of risk.

The Account will ordinarily be invested principally in a diversified portfolio of marketable common stocks and other marketable equity-type investments, including but not limited to convertible bonds and convertible preferred stocks. The Account may also hold cash, short-term obligations, and U.S. Government, corporate, and other bonds.

Or more simply:

The investment goal of this portfolio will be total return, capital and income, and it is understood that in order to achieve this goal, we may take risks commensurate with the potential gains.

In addition to the objectives, there may be a list of restrictions:

1. No purchase of (company) securities except to the extent that such securities may be an incidental part of a mutual fund in which investments are made.
2. No loans to (company).
3. No financial dealings with any subsidiaries, or affiliates of (company).
4. No loans to (company) officers or employees.
5. No puts, calls, strips, or straddles.
6. No short sales.
7. No letter stocks.
8. No investments for purpose of exercising control over management, and no more than a 5 percent holding of the sum of voting and nonvoting stock of one firm.
9. No investments in private placement bonds or direct real-estate investments, except to the extent that such investments may be part of a mutual fund in which investments are made.
10. No more than 20 percent of current market value in securities of one firm.

11. No more than 20 percent of assets under management to be invested in companies that, together with predecessor companies, have been in operation less than five years.
12. No more than 20 percent of assets in foreign securities, subject to the further marketability restrictions in (8).

Objectives may inherently reflect the market environment in which they were written; for example, one company stated their objectives to us as follows:

"The objectives of the (company) pension fund should be determined by the long-term nature of the liabilities involved. Appropriate objectives are:

1. To preserve the capital value of fund assets
2. To have sufficient liquidity to meet projected disbursements without forcing the fund managers to liquidate holdings in bad markets
3. To earn a rate of return on the equity portion of fund assets 10 percent better than the S & P 500 in up markets and at least equal it in down markets
4. To earn an overall rate of return between 8-11 percent over time (assuming annual inflation of less than 5 percent)
5. To reduce the volatility of the fund"

Some objectives grow out of the almost desperate needs of investors. Schools, hit early with rising costs and lower federal funding, were among the most pressed to project their needs onto investment attainment. One of the best efforts to increase endowment returns was made by a school that discussed its investment objectives in a report to the trustees as follows:

"The Ford Foundation report articulated an investment concept that, in fact, [school] has been following for many years. Ford suggested that, rather than viewing portfolio performance solely in terms of the dividend- and interest-income produced, the appreciation (or depreciation) in principal values should also be considered. The implication of this concept is that universities should not necessarily limit their spending to the income portion of their portfolio, but should also rely in a prudent and measured way on capital appreciation of the portfolio. In seeking to develop a portfolio performance goal for [school] based on this total return concept, this Board gave deep thought both to [school's] needs and to feasible and historic portfolio results.

"To summarize these deliberations of two years ago—particularly for those who did not participate—our consideration of [school's] needs suggested that operating deficits were likely to continue, thereby indicating a need for *some* reliance on the principal portion of our endowment fund for current operations. (These operating deficits are not unique to [school], as we all know. In *Harvard and Money* the authors estimated that Harvard's operating budget will double by 1980, raising the prospect of serious deficits in that well-endowed institution.) In addition to an expanding operating budget, [school] faces significant capital investment requirements. And, despite a planned major capital fund drive, it is clear that [school's] endowment will be called on in some measure to meet these capital needs. The net of these two factors, when priced out with detailed budgets and capital spending projections, suggested that a 12 percent return from [school's] portfolio—allowing for a reasonable amount of inflation—was clearly needed to maintain the economic viability of the institution.

"In testing the feasibility of realizing an average annual return of 12 percent, the Board considered evidence presented in the University of Chicago's study* indicating that long-term total returns from randomly selected com-

---

* L. Fisher, and James Lorie, "Rates of Returns on Investments in Common Stocks (1926-1965) ," *The Journal of Business* of the Graduate School of Business, University of Chicago, July 1968.

mon stocks have averaged approximately 9 percent annually over a 40-year period. As many of you will recall, we reasoned that if this kind of return was a historical fact in unmanaged portfolios, a professionally managed fund should exceed this result by a substantial margin. We also concluded that professional management of our portfolio should yield us an even greater margin when compared to investment alternatives in either fixed income securities or thrift institutions. (This is not to suggest that under certain market conditions fixed income securities would not be an attractive alternative for [school's] fund managers, from both income and capital appreciation standpoints.)

"As a further check on our thinking, we researched quite carefully the publicly available data on the performance of many mutual funds. Here we found evidence that over five-, ten-, and even fifteen-year periods, average returns on the order of 12 percent had been realized. And, during our recent interviews with prospective nonbank fund managers, we developed some corroborating evidence that astute professional management could, in fact, provide [school] with an average total return of 12 percent over the long term.

"In summary, if the endowment is to fulfill the demands that we believe the [school] will have to make on it, it must substantially outperform the market averages over the long term, and we believe that this not only must be done but that—with proper management—it can be done."

Yield

Investing for yield attempts to optimize current return. Many institutions today, like colleges and foundations, have a growing need for current operating funds. Despite the fact that they believe that increased market value averaged over a time is a meaningful measure, few institutions feel comfortable for very long in the old-fashioned "spending of capital." They are a lot happier with a high current return and are attracted to yield-oriented portfolios. Individuals have always liked a dividend check coming in now and then. Changes in the market price of a portfolio have always seemed a bit ethereal to individual investors, whereas a tangible check in the hand is evidence that the company's investment is working out. Increases in dividends were one of the things to which an individual was most responsive. It suggested that the company's fortunes were improving far more than just reports of higher income per share.

The individual investor may look at the total dollars he receives as a return from his investment portfolio, computing the yield based on market price. Individual investors frequently figure yield on cost price. This is not a bad notion as long as one uses it to examine the performance record of previous decisions rather than determining a basis for new decisions. The best way to invest for yield may be to look at high-income securities to see whether the income level suffices for whatever one's individual forecast about future inflation may be or to examine the rates of increases of past dividends.

One can use dividend trends as one might employ a trend line of earnings per share. The traditional method of obtaining high portfolio yields is to invest a portion of an account in cash or fixed income securities, which produce a higher yield than equities. After the entire income requirement is derived from those sources, the remainder of the portfolio is invested in appreciation-oriented equities. Such a balance may have been more appropriate when it was a novel suggestion than currently when so many portfolios have implemented this strategy. Use of this strategy is why income securities may be more underpriced relative to the total market than securities that were purchased for appreciation. If growth stocks are overpriced, they have already been discounted.

One of the principal objectives of investing for yield may be to uphold the purchasing power of the income dollar. Few institutional investors plot the increase in income stream as an objective when analyzing portfolio performance. There is an excellent argument that such an income stream, with an almost complete disregard of the capital value, is a valid investment objective. Individual investors, as we have already stated, tend to look at their portfolio performance by growth of income stream as well as changes in capital value. Growth in dividends has been a good inflation hedge. The income stream produced by the S & P 500 increased at a 4.4 percent annual rate between 1964 and 1974.

Corporate attitudes toward dividends are critical when determining a company's dividend policy. Dividends are difficult to pay out, since they must be produced from after-tax earnings. In no way can a company directly get the dividends back in the event it needs additional financial strength for difficult days. A cash-rich company like General Motors has few aggressive opportunities because of its already dominant market share in the automotive industry. It has determined, however, based upon an imputed examination of its dividend practice, to pay out approximately 50 percent of earnings in a trough of the business cycle. For earnings that can be attributed to an expansion in demand above trough, it has determined to pay out 80 percent of these extraordinary gains, usually in the form of an extra.

In this way the company maintains financial strength and still rewards its shareholders for the excellent business conditions it may enjoy. Most companies seem to have a more simplistic payout formula, usually as a percentage of reported earnings. Because reported earnings have recently been liberalized for shareholder-reporting purposes and reported earnings increased, the payout was dropped. A typical disbursement may be expected to be somewhat less now than ten years ago.

Corporate liquidity has declined. Cash as a percentage of total assets currently is slightly less than a decade ago, and corporate borrowings are up. The reconciliation of these figures suggests that the residual of retained earnings had to be committed to replace capital assets at higher costs rather than to support new business. Some reported earnings were not available for distribution, although it is normally expected by investors that all of reported income, assuming that a company wished to establish such a policy, could be paid out as cash to the shareholders.

Corporations occasionally use dividends to attract shareholder loyalty at a time when it might otherwise be criticized. U.S. Industries raised its dividend in 1974 in the face of declining earnings when management was plagued by suits from dissident shareholders and division heads. The increase was followed quickly by the withdrawal of a commercial-paper rating by Moody's, based in part upon the results of an unconsolidated finance subsidiary. One can surmise that the dividend increase was used as a shareholder bribe. Utilities have raised dividends coincident with higher borrowings and rising capital costs.

Statistically, one of the most responsive causal items between stock-price performance and fundamentals is the dividend increase. If one could accurately forecast such increases, it would be possible to marginally outperform the market. Most institutional analysts, however, by spending all of their time in attempting to forecast earnings per share in an environment that does not give credit to dividends, scarcely attempt to forecast the timing or extent of dividend increases.

I suggest that such an effort is possible and rewarding. Increasingly, investors will be investing for yield. In an inflationary environment, they will be interested in the type of yield that grows, rather than remains static, as in a bond or preferred stock. Just as company managements tend to persist with successful management decisions if they are good, so do investors reveal consistent patterns for dividend increases.

One must remember that dividends are paid out of cash and not necessarily out of earnings. However, a low payout in relationship to past historical norms—that is, a low ratio of current dividends to earnings—is a strong indication that a change may be pending. A company whose working capital has steadily increased at the same time that earnings have increased is an especially likely candidate for a dividend change.

Companies also tend to make dividend decisions on a seasonal pattern. Dividends are likely to be increased at the same time each year, in combination with the company's own forecasting cycle. In the past decade, dividends have not advanced at the same rate as earnings, reflecting in part the fact that not all earnings have been translated into cash and that companies have needed a higher proportion of net income to replace plant and equipment.

It is critical for a company to avoid dividend cuts. There is probably no greater evidence of a company's deterioration than a reduction in its payment to shareholders. This is an extreme position, taken very reluctantly and usually under pressure from outside lenders, indicative that the company has exhausted its borrowing reserve. Deteriorating earnings are the principal sign, but more directly one can look in the balance sheet for bank covenants and the amount of retained earnings that are available for the payment of dividends. These reflect the degree of harshness and concern the commercial banker is imposing upon the company.

It has been my impression that companies with commercial bankers on the board may be slightly quicker to cut their dividends than those without. Once a major institutional security cuts its dividend, a process of exchange of hands of nearly the entire capitalization begins, during which several years of poor stock prices will follow. Almost regardless of the price to which the stock falls early after a dividend cut, one can expect a long time of disappointing price performance from a major income-producing security.

The best example recently is an entirely new industry that grew up as an income-producing vehicle. The real-estate investment trusts were granted conduit status by the Internal Revenue Service in the early sixties. As such, they paid no corporate tax as long as they paid over 90 percent of their earnings to shareholders. And yet these companies were a financing vehicle, just like mortgage bankers or banks. In fact, banks were providing the principal source of funds to the real-estate investment trusts. A $4 billion industry grew up that served to take money from large institutional investors, essentially banks and insurance companies, and later corporations through commercial paper, and to lend this money for construction and development loans.

The average maturity of the loan by the real-estate investment trust was longer than its borrowings. As such, the real-estate investment trust was borrowing short and lending long—a prescription for indigestion when money tightened. Nevertheless, the underlying security became a progressively more attractive income vehicle. Real-estate investment trust prices started at something slightly over book value; as they added leverage on top of the equity, they sold at two to three times book value. Subsequent issues of equity at the market price increased this value because the company could take the premium it received over book and add leverage on top of that inflated price. It was a great scheme, so long as business conditions were conducive to the industry it served—the housing industry. Lenders were willing to lend to progressively marginal companies in the field, and investors recognized that they had vehicles for income and not appreciation. A number of these securities were sold to dividend-hungry people, and the industry records of dividend growth were quite phenomenal.

In the latter part of 1972, one began to notice items in the press where various real-estate investment trusts advertised proudly that they had been able to place some of their money in real-estate projects around the country. One advertised pride in its ability to spend money. One could assume that the field became overcrowded. There was more money available than projects and some loans were of low quality.

Despite this reasonably simplistic observation, dividends still increased and stocks continued to rise. Major brokerage houses had teams of two or three people following the industry. The securities were also found in portfolios of individuals and institutions who bought them because they thought that others, wanting income, would pay progressively higher prices to maintain the yield level as dividends were raised.

As many know, dividend cuts became rampant throughout the industry in 1973. First, many loans went sour and stocks plummeted as dividends were cut. At one time during 1973–1974, the securities in this industry sold at two times earnings, yields on past norms indicating cuts yet to come of 30 to 50 percent. Some stocks in the industry fell to zero as companies went bankrupt or their loans were called.

Income-oriented investors had to sell these stocks out of their portfolios, so they felt, at any price. The price declines were the most vicious I have ever observed, especially when one considers that if the projects were correctly appraised in the first place and were foreclosed, a mortgage-holding trust might now be attractive for quite different purposes; that is, it could be an equity trust by changing its charter. Metropolitan Life Insurance Company foreclosed on many farms during the Great Depression, but became a large landholder and later established the base for its insurance growth. The morals of looking at the real-estate investment trusts are severalfold: (1) avoid dividend cuts; (2) be careful of leverage working against you; (3) yet to be proven, don't be too hasty in determining what business your company may be in.

Profit

There is a European investment axiom: "Buy assets, sell earnings." This implies that one should buy potentially productive, but not currently earning, assets and sell them when they are appraised on the basis of their earnings. Many European merchant bankers traditionally make this sort of investment. They buy for their private account asset-oriented companies that may be in trouble. They place management to improve the situation and then distribute the companies to the public when they can be priced on an earnings basis.

In the American market the price to book value relationship has averaged about 2.0 times in the post-World War II period, suggesting that the stock market is priced on the basis of earnings and not assets. More recently, in late 1974, this ratio fell on the average stock to below book. With an average close to book value and with book value understated, it is possible to find in the American market (for the first time in over a decade) many opportunities where one can apply the canny European investment styles. I have suggested to several Europeans that the foreign investor may be more successful in the American market than his native counterpart. He should utilize his European techniques and not try to imitate, which I believe most do, what they think of as sophisticated American investment strategy.

Investing for gain seems to be everyone's goal. During the two-and-a-half decade bull market that ended in 1966, investing for gain seemed quite easy. While the analogy of the Random Walk Theory dart board has been overdone, it was appropriate, particularly in hindsight. Since then, any one who has produced and maintained an investment gain either has been very lucky or unusually skillful.

Individual investors usually have very modest appreciation objectives. Except for wild trading practices in the hope of producing instant profit late in the bull market, individual investors appear to invest in value-oriented securities, anticipating that their assets would adjust to the inflation rate, but they recognize that they will not get rich from this procedure. Most do not keep careful records; they don't know from one year to the next what the gain has been.

Individual investors know that they produce a loss if the security sells below cost or if there has been a dramatic price change. Many individuals have in their portfolios some of the popular glamour stocks, such as Polaroid or IBM, at very low tax cost. These securities were bought in a diversified portfolio back in the fifties by more venturesome investors; of course, their tax cost is only a few dollars a share. Investors in Polaroid who have seen the stock as high as $169 a share are well aware that they have lost money at a market price of $20, although their tax cost may still be lower than the current market.

Institutions tend to be more impressed with investing for gain. In the first place, they keep shorter-term accounting records and respond with enthusiasm or dismay whenever there is a change of market value in a large portfolio. At Keystone, daily portfolio pricing sheets were distributed to portfolio managers at the end of the day and each manager considered we made or lost whatever million dollars profit or gain occurred from the preceding day. This response to essentially nonsensical short-term information built into one's system a myopic attitude to the time horizon in which a security was expected to perform.

Institutional portfolios tend to be slightly more volatile than the market, suggesting that, in converse, individual portfolios should be slightly less volatile. On good days in the market an institutional portfolio could be expected to go up more and on bad days it would go down more. Most institutions are oriented toward doing well in a bull market. Indeed, that is when there is the greatest attention to see whether or not one is keeping pace. A bear market is expected, by the institutional frame of mind, to be of short duration and not too significant for investment-trading purposes. On the contrary, there have been as many bear market months as bull-market months in the five years 1969 through 1974. So it seemed from the price behavior of the average stock. In fact, the Dow Jones Industrial Average declined 30 out of 60 months in 1969 to 1973—a 50 percent record.

There is a strong tendency for institutional portfolios to increase their volatility; that is, to buy riskier securities as the market rises. The more stable, defensive securities do well enough in a bull-market period but appear to fall behind the more exciting investments of one's competitors. To the extent that competitive performance establishes the base by which institutions are measured, there is an almost irresistible tendency to take higher degrees of risk as the market pace accelerates.

There is an almost equally strong tendency to reduce volatility as the market declines. Thus, at the top of the market, an institutional portfolio would have its maximum degree of risk volatility and its lowest at the bottom. An appropriate investment strategy, investing for optimum gain, would stress the converse. As the market rises, one should, on a mechanical basis, reduce volatility and make less risky investments. As the market recedes, one should increase the risk so that at the very bottom the risk is close to maximum.

A decade or more ago, bank trust departments were nearly the ideal depository for assets. Banks could be counted upon to be the conservators. They would accept the management of portfolios, maintain the holdings in only the highest quality bonds and stocks, and make very few decisions. Banks would give an investor a "piece of the rock" without pretense that there would be large gains or high performance. This was especially appropriate for the very large sums attracted to banks and trust companies.

The pressure from clients for more gains, coupled with bank managements wanting to find a reason to increase their fees, pulled and pushed bank operations into the performance race in the late sixties. The banks suddenly tried to imitate mutual funds with portfolio razzle-dazzle, topnotch people, and an investment style that was out of date by the time they adopted it. In a business sense, this change left large opportunities for traditional consevators of assets but these opportunities have not yet been fully recognized.

More importantly, the conversion of bankers to traders is a glaring example of institutional investors putting their own needs ahead of those of their clients. The clients' large pension and endowment funds did not need, in fact could not achieve, for the sums in their possession, the gains promised by institutions. They could have reached their goals more easily by continuing in the low-cost conservatory mood of the fifties and sixties.

The capital-gains tax structure is a major hindrance for any individual investor who strives to achieve portfolio gain. In the first place, there is evidence that "countertrend" strategy is more appropriate in order to maximize gain. It is better to accept profits when you have them, which means establishing a capital gain and reinvesting the proceeds in securities that have underperformed those you elected to sell. When an individual follows this procedure, he must pay a capital-gains tax. This leaves him with less to reinvest than he had originally, for his asset base is eroded by the amount of the tax. In part, the individual investor does faulty accounting to the extent that he computes his net worth based upon full market value of the securities. He does not put aside something to offset accrued capital-gains taxes, and figures his profit in terms of market prices with no thought of Uncle Sam.

The capital-gains tax is in effect a no-interest loan from the government, tied to a specific piece of collateral. To consider that it is part of the investor's net worth, as is usually done, results in some very faulty decisions and may be one of the reasons for the stock market's very low liquidity in the early seventies.

Few individual investors have been happy with the tax-shelter investments they have undertaken. I have looked at many real-estate, oil-drilling, and cattle deals for investors and have seen few that should be undertaken were it not for special tax features. In general, this is an area that has been exploited only by the very wealthy who have battalions of specialists structuring deals especially for them. They have a continuing employment relationship with the people who put the deals together. By the time tax-shelter deals are put out on a merchant basis to a sales force, the individual investor has cause to be very wary of the prospective investment result.

Growth

I once was interviewed by a reporter new to the investment field who asked: "What are the objectives of your clients?" I replied, "Total return, a combination of income and appreciation, without taking excessive risk of loss."

The reporter asked again, "Oh, appreciation means you buy growth stocks?" "No," I said, "we don't buy growth stocks because so many people have bought stocks associated with growth of earnings that they have already discounted, in our opinion, more than the prospect of the earnings growth, which was supposed to enhance the price."

"Hmm, you want growth of capital but you don't buy growth stocks. I don't understand."

The exchange, which actually went on in three, different, ten-minute segments spread throughout a two-hour interview, illustrated to me the confusion between growth in stock selection and growth as a portfolio objective. Growth as it relates to the nature of a company of a type of earnings pattern may be quite similar to portfolio growth, which may be achieved by a variety of different methods.

Confusion caused by the use of the same word for means and ends has established a number of suspiciously unattractive investment procedures. It may well be, in fact recently has been, a far better way of achieving portfolio growth to invest in high-income securities and to pursue an active trading policy than to buy premier growth favorites that have already been identified by most as the best institutional universe.

It may be that the best way to achieve investment growth is to alternate between high risk and low risk at various points of a market cycle. One way to identify different points of the market cycle is to examine one's own investment experience. If, after a period, results have been very successful, one can assume he is not at the beginning of a bull market, but somewhere along in the rise. Correspondingly, if growth stocks have declined sharply in terms of market price, it does not mean necessarily that these companies have ceased to be good growth vehicles.

A strange phenomenon is occurring now, and much discussion is taking place within academic and investment circles about the implications of Zero Population Growth (ZPG) on the investment structure. It may well be, some would argue, that growth itself is no longer a principal objective of companies; moreover, it may change as an objective for portfolios. Perhaps, as most companies had a 15 percent compound growth-rate objective in the sixties and portfolios had similar or greater objectives, we will move to a base where growth itself is not highly prized, but qualitative factors, perhaps containing the ingredients of social re sponsibility, will be prized. That is, companies that provide attractive environments for their employees and do not pollute the air and the sea or that are innovative in providing useful cultural services for the country will become prized more for these characteristics than for growth of profits. Discussions regarding zero-growth are so embryonic that it is difficult to quantify the terms that may be used. However, I suspect that considerations of this sort will become commonplace in future investment portfolios.

Another implication of the zero-growth argument for investors is that a company must be aggressive, assertive, and competitive within its field if it expects to grow in an essentially nonexpanding environment. Certain companies are growth companies that have been swept along within a growth industry. Some of the second-grade computer companies had these characteristics, in that the growth of the industry was perhaps being sponsored by IBM and a few others. But a number of weak companies had, for a while, growth characteristics and were being propelled forward by the activities of someone else.

To the other extreme, there are weak companies in nongrowth industries, like steel and railroad. Such industries have long since stopped growing. Being no longer competitive, they have accepted a docile role of survivorship and mediocrity.

In between are companies in industries formerly

growing but now static, where competitive pressures forced the companies to knock each other off. Home-building and building-materials companies are examples in this type of industry environment. There is perhaps no industry more closely tied to general population growth and prosperity than the housing industry. As both features seem to wane in importance, housing starts—cyclical anyway—have plummeted. Pricing pressures have forced home-building companies into precarious financial conditions, and among the raw-material-oriented companies, building materials have been the weakest so far in the early seventies.

Strong industries are those that by definition are growing at a rate in excess of the economy, presumably at least twice as fast. The economy was growing on the order of 5 percent. This might be a combination of 3 percent real growth and 2 percent GNP deflator. Now it is growing at 1 to 2 percent real growth and 7 or 8 percent GNP deflator, for a total of 10 percent. Industries doing respectively double these figures could be classified as growth industries.

Inflation

For some time since World War II, inflation has been a principal stimulus to investment by individuals. Of course, the primary purpose in investing has been necessity. Either saving for future consumption was required or surplus funds had to be invested. In either case, the investment funds were those for which one individual would forego consumption and transfer to another who required them for current consumption.

The funds were still used to support the current economy, but one man's saving was converted to an investment in another man's consumption, which was greater than his original means. When the process reverses and there is a reduction in the investment, the second man, who is the recipient of the investment in the first instance, foregoes consumption in order to pay off his debt. The acceptance of the paid-off debt means that the first man presumably now wishes to consume. In both cases consumption levels are identical. There is merely a shift in asset ownership.

Inflation has been generally accelerating since the depression. There have been periods of very low inflation levels under artificial price-control conditions or when the economy operated below capacity. But in general in this economic cycle as with most others of history, inflation rates move up until there is massive debt liquidation, a war, or a depression.

The shift from bonds to stocks, which took place in investment portfolios in the mid to late fifties and early sixties, was precipitated by interest rate increases that reduced the capital value of bond portfolios and accompanied a rising stock market. This attracted investors to downgrade their investment quality, in a classical sense, in order to protect the purchasing power of their funds. They did not acaccept one other technique traditionally used by individuals for protecting purchasing power: converting funds into purchased goods that may be needed in the future. The American consumer has always responded to higher prices by withholding funds from consumption or by saving until conditions improve, although the decision is not especially economic. The European consumer, on the other hand, has responded to uncertainty in the past by spending while he has the chance and before prices go higher.

In the mid seventies for the first time the American consumer began to behave like his European counterpart. Inflation rates are common ingredients in the pricing of both bonds and stocks. Bonds, earlier studies show, have traditionally been priced at approximately 12 percent, 3 percent real return, plus an increment for the imbedded rate of inflation, or the rate of inflation expected by investors over the period for which the bonds would be held. So although a bond may yield 10 percent to maturity, this implies an expected inflation rate of approximately 8 percent per year, with a residual real return of money of approximately 2 percent.

The real return will be realized to the extent to which the bond is paid off, and the expected inflation rate is close to actual for the period to be covered. Similarly, equities are priced according to some notion of real growth which, if exactly the same as the economy, might be in the 2 to 3 percent region, plus a discount rate applied to future earnings of the expected rate of inflation. Presumably the inflation rate is the same as that applied to bonds, if bonds and stocks are being priced by the same universe of investors.

There is an unusual offset, however, in that equities represent a call on real assets, which are the basis for producing earnings on capital. Moreover, the typical American company has an equity-debt ratio of four to one and essentially is borrowing in current dollars and converting to real assets for payment in future dollars. There is some factor to be subtracted from the discount rate of inflation on future earnings, since an equity in an inflationary environment reflects somewhat greater value. This is due to the fact that U.S. corporations are net borrowers, and that real assets are likely to be appreciating in current-dollar terms.

This discount factor varies according to the nature of the corporation, but in every case it will be more than zero. Therefore, the discount rate applied to future earnings is something less than that applied to bonds. The only bond adjustment factor, beyond that of uncertainty, is the possibility of higher interest rates creating a better reinvestment opportunity for the current income produced by bonds. The higher the reinvestment rate is than the original rate, the lower the capital value is from what had been estimated, assuming the interest rate is greater because of inflation or a deterioration in credit of quality.

An examination of market periods in Europe, Japan, and the United States in which inflation rates have doubled —that is, increased from 2 to 4 percent, or 3 to 6 percent, or the like—suggests that inflation is a neutral to mildly positive influence on equity prices, although not directly coincident with stock prices except during the late stage blow-off period. Under these conditions when people treat cash as a hot potato, they use the stock market as a readily available device to increase the velocity of investment funds. We all know that there is nothing like a bull market to use up funds very quickly. When inflation in Germany approximated 1,000 percent between mid 1923 and 1924, its stock market appreciated commensurately, although business conditions were bad.

Inflation inserts a new item of uncertainty into business decision-making. With fluctuating prices of raw materials, labor, and services, businessmen respond to the uncertainty by building up profit-margin safeguards. Usually, in a nonprice-controlled environment, these safeguards are more than adequate for the demands being placed upon the income statement. For example, the recession of early 1974 was the first post-World War II recession in which corporate profits rose. Although the recession was accompanied by a virulent period of price increases, those securities in industries like oil, in which price rises had been most pronounced, were similarly those companies that had the greatest increase in corporate profits. Businessmen responded to the uncertainty about pricing at their own retail end.

Inflation may make business decision-making more difficult, but there is little evidence that it makes it less successful from a profit-margin standpoint. To be sure, profits, if adjusted on a real basis, may decline when business declines. That would be expected in any normal business cycle. However, the definition of inflation is a period of price increases. Although perhaps lagging somewhat through the industrial cycle, the cost of raw materials is generally an adjustment to allow profits to be made under the new business conditions.

The investments that most of us will recognize sell on a basis in some way comparable to their profit-making potential. In an overall profits rise, one would expect that investments would also rise. Thus, one can see that a period of price improvement is not essentially harmful for equities, but perhaps mildly beneficial.

6

The Role of
Institutions

Education of an Institutional Investor

A great deal of what happens in the investment world involves persuading someone to do something he would not do had your persuasion not worked. Brokers sell securities to investors. Investors persuade other investors that the securities they own will be profitable. Investment managers persuade clients that they can do better than the market averages, and clients persuade themselves, in some cases, that they can become rich through the investment process.

There are three forms of persuasion: (1) the presentation of facts, which when revealed will indicate that a certain course of action must be taken; (2) obscuring facts that may be contrary to the action that one wishes another person to take; (3) the more subtle form of reallocating weights given to components of the decision-making that one wishes another person to make. Most persuasion is directed toward self-serving commercial interest: trying to get somebody to do something that will enhance one's own financial status or well-being.

Occasionally one will find a higher form of persuasion—the expression of the professional view that someone
else should do something that may not be in the best financial interest of the individual giving the advice.

My first experience with salesmanship at a workaday
level occurred between my sophomore and junior year at
Harvard, well before I thought of the investment business.
The year was 1953 and the Vick Chemical Company, manufacturers of Vapo-Rub (or salve, as it was called in the
South) and other cold products, customarily recruited
twenty-five "eager beavers" from college campuses around
the country.

The recruiting lure was sales training as a traveling
salesman working for a large and sophisticated marketing
company with full expenses paid and a chance to clear the
salary of $25 a week. This program had its own illustrious
alumni, who were currently engaged in high-level positions
in marketing companies. Anyone who seriously wanted to
consider a field in marketing entered this competition. The
ingredients of selection were those factors that Vick considered important for future executive training as well as
a good sales presence.

Since I was considering a career in some field of business and knew that salesmanship would be part of almost
any activity, I applied for the program. Interviews were held
at half-hour intervals in the college placement office. My interview was conducted by an affable Yale-like member of
the personnel department named Thomas Buffum. In the
course of one preliminary interview and a later visit to the
company, he gave me the impression we were friends.

I was selected from among hundreds who applied and
eagerly looked forward to a different summer-job experience. The program encompassed ten weeks. The first week
we reported to the George Washington Hotel on lower Fifth
Avenue, a low-cost hostelry that was convenient to the compa-

ny's marketing headquarters in New York City. People came from all over the country and were a blend of all the types of students that one would find in a cross section of the college population. They were quick, social, ambitious—more likely to be officers of their social fraternities than scholars, but they were not an unintelligent group.

The week's program was conducted by the sales-training department, the same group that does the indoctrination programs for full-time marketing people at Vick. Essentially, we were trained in the general concept that the druggists and wholesalers whom we were to meet in a sales situation were our enemies. Our task was to have a mentally combative frame of mind if we were to achieve victory in our contest with the sales prospects. There was no conviction expressed that we were there to do public service by bringing Vick goods to these needy retailers at special summer rates. We were here to put goods on the shelf and, having succeeded at that, to place prominently an unattractive point-of-sale placard showing a female model with a finger beside one nostril and a Vick's inhaler in the other. During the week we sang Vick songs and drank Vick cocktails (gin and cough syrup) and were finally launched on our venture by an evangelistic message from the president of the company.

I was sent to Baltimore for several days of on-the-spot indoctrination before going to my sales territory. I had been assigned a rented car and a sample kit in New York, and sent on my way. My ultimate assignment was the southern half of Georgia, Alabama, and Mississippi, territories, which, for understandable reasons in the pre-automotive air-conditioning days, the regular salesmen were reluctant to cover.

In Baltimore I met a veteran salesman who was on his way north with the birds for the season. We made a few calls together in Baltimore while I listened to what he had to say to the druggist. "Hello, Mr. Druggist. My name is John Smith, and I'm here to tell you about the special opportunity available to acquire your profitable winter needs at a price that will help you make more money than you have ever before," and so on. These calls while I was a passive assistant—the obvious junior apprentice—were like the smell of battle. They further goaded one to a feverish pitch and reminded me again of the inspirational words of the president, explaining how small ideas could help make the company make the man who had them. He has used the example of the man who discovered that by widening the mouth of the large economy-sized Vapo-Rub, the average consumer would use three fingers to apply the salve, thereby increasing the wastage by 50 percent.

I was anxious to solo. After making a few dual calls, where I initiated the conversation, I still had the salesman standing by looking on like the teacher. From earlier sales reports an easy prospect was selected. We were in the slums of Baltimore, and sales figures on a very small drugstore indicated that it had been a steady annual purchaser of Vick's products. With my new sample case and order pad and pen ready—even with a ratchet screwdriver which I bought with my own money to quickly install the point-of-sales sign before someone had second thoughts—I assaulted the door.

I entered the small, poor drugstore and went immediately to the back of it as my training had taught me to do. I met an elderly couple and began my pitch. "Mr. Druggist, I'm here to help you acquire your stock of profitable Vick's products." The elderly couple continued to have a bemused expression throughout the pitch, although as I progressed toward what we call the "Oh, my God" size deal, I noticed that they were ready to buy, although the shelves I could see within my range of vision seemed to be adequately supplied. It occurred to me that they were not very intelligent. I broke off my spiel and asked a few questions and discovered that this nice old couple was deaf. Apparently their shelves had been more than adequately supplied by wholesalers who came along and took care of them in a fashion somewhat similar to the stocking of a blind newsdealer.

It was quite clear that they were ready to sign whatever order form I put in front of them, which, if they did, would have resulted in great praise from my teacher waiting in the car, and my release as a certified summer salesman to take over my own territory. On the other hand, they did not, as near as I could tell, need the goods. I could go back and explain that they were adequately stocked and had no further need of Vick's services for the coming year. Furthermore, they didn't understand a word I was saying.

Under those circumstances, I would go back to the grueling job of making several more dual calls on the presumption I had crashed on my solo flight and, at the very least, had lost my nerve. The moral of the dilemma was clear, and the decision I made then has affected my attitudes on persuasion ever since.

Few can understand now why I have been especially decisive in declining business opportunities that had attractive short-run possibilities but were of doubtful long-run value. I have felt that brokers had as much obligation in serving their clients to recommend the sale of securities that they felt lacked merit as to recommend their purchase. I have recommended to some investment management clients that they look for other good firms when their interests do not coincide with our capabilities. These acts are not the expressions of someone who is intentionally shortsighted commercially, but rather the result of decision-making by one who has returned to Baltimore many times looking for a small drugstore in the hope that he could buy back the $500 worth of Vick's products that must still be on the shelves.

My father was a doctor, who aspired that his son

would work in the same profession by getting a better education than he had been able to afford during the depression years. I had no problem with this, but the sight of blood made me think of a butcher shop. He sacrificed enough to send me to the best private schools in the hope that I would see the wisdom of his view. Attendance at medical meetings and at surgical amphitheaters confirmed in my head and stomach that the decision to pass up medicine was correct.

I was excessively well prepared for Harvard and proceeded to play during my first two years there. I was nearly thrown out of college for majoring in girls, bottles, and planes, rather than books. The academic jolt was timely and useful. My last two years were spent seriously studying psychology and sociology rather than the typical premed program of biochemistry less suited to my personal aspirations.

I then spent one year working for a New England manufacturer, Norton Company, in its personnel section, and two years in the Army, during most of which I was stationed in Germany. I was fortunate there in being assigned to run psychological tests for the leadership training of noncommissioned officers under the scientific and professional personnel program.

When I had left college I decided to go to the Harvard Business School and undertake training leading me to a career in labor relations. The labor ferment of the fifties had been presold in my mind and my generally liberal leanings superimposed on the background of a fairly conservative education seemed to suit me for the middle ground as a negotiator. Harvard Business School had been reluctant to take me right out of school and a fairly checkered academic career. They were more inclined to accept my application when I visited the Admissions Office during a break from the Placement Office, where I was hiring members of that year's graduating class for my employer.

The draft notice took precedence, but I came back to the Harvard Business School in September 1958 to begin my career in labor work. Several books have been written about the Harvard Business School and business-school experiences in general, but few have captured the intensity of the early weeks.

You start with a class of approximately 600 highly motivated, aggressive, competitive students. They all recognize that they are taking time out from other activities that might be quite valuable, and they want to utilize this time very effectively. The first nine weeks between September and Thanksgiving are similar to a marine boot camp. The work is piled on and one's entire career at the Business School and, by inference, much of one's business career, is shaped in this relatively short time.

If you are fortunate enough to room with a good student with a competitive spirit, as I was,* you are helped immeasurably. If you are with a more lackadaisical group, you may not get going at full speed at the beginning. Case assignments are issued, papers are assigned, and the work progresses seven days a week. I did little else but read, write, and study for the first two months.

I followed the premise that success at the Harvard Business School depends not only upon intelligence but upon the ability to persuade others of your view. It is intended to be an intensive business experience. Students were as much aware of the need for cooperation as the need for competition. It was a forum in many respects like Congress, where beneath the surface of respect and comradery rest the hard attitudes that realize the doorway of success is too narrow to accommodate all who have the ability to pass through.

---

* John G. L. Cabot, now Vice President, Energy Group, Cabot Corporation, manufacturers of carbon black and energy products.

One particularly fiendish method of training was the Saturday-night paper, called written analysis of cases (WAC). The cases were ostensibly to improve one's writing ability, but they served a far more important function in establishing a requirement to complete an assignment that could draw upon one's earlier education and training, like English composition. The cases were read by intelligent young women who were recent college graduates. One of my section-mates was an intensive Englishman with an athletic build, who, trying to make the 9 P.M. deadline, collapsed and had to be hospitalized once while racing to the chute in which papers were placed from his typist, who was located two miles away on the other side of Harvard Square.

About 200 of my classmates were interested in the investment business and one of the most popular courses was Leonard Langer's course on investments. This was typical of a period of great prosperity and a bull market—clearly not the case today. Those who were not interested in some area of the investment field enrolled in the course on new enterprise.

For some years, the investment business was not considered to be a very critical profession. Certainly, during the depression years it was not a place where a young man sought to win his fortune. During World War II, brokers had the lowest possible exemption—in other words, it was a least critical industry for the war effort.

Following the war, a few people came back into the investment business; perhaps their experience had been either in the finance or payroll sections of the military. The basis of this experience was rather unstable. Many brokers seemed to get into the investment business because some had experience with wealth in their families. It was an appropriate place to park the second or third son after religion, education, or law had absorbed the elder, or more qualified, sons.

Most investment people in the early postwar period

ventured into the business by chance. Those who succeeded most were sales-oriented marketing people who would have done well in any business. It was hard to sell securities in those low-volume years. It required effort and push. The institutions what were on the rise were mutual funds. As the twenty-five-year bull market progressed in the 1950's, young men increasingly eager for riches looked to finance, whether in the corporate or investment area.

The investment course at Harvard Business School was for businessmen who might have to face the problem of investing their own funds later on, rather than for those who were going to undertake a professional investment career. There was a legendary character, Mrs. Heald, a widow, who had a variety of investment problems. These were handled in a paper-portfolio sense by students. It was not so much a course to pick stocks that would move up, since Mrs. Heald was very conservative and would have unusual cash-flow problems as the term progressed. Mrs. Heald communicated directly with each student in the course, as the students would communicate with her. It was indeed an exercise in handholding as well as in the design of a personal investment portfolio. It did seem incongruous, however, that most of us were dealing with the problems involving widows. It seemed about as far removed from what we might be doing with our own portfolio as could be imagined.

The first year course at the Business School is general and prescribed. The courses cover production, marketing, business policy, and the like. It is a general grounding on all the aspects of business that might be encountered. It was during this period that I became especially interested in finance. It occurred in the way in which most students fall into a subject—influence of my teachers. The instructors in the finance area were particularly striking. They seemed to grasp the whole sweep of business problems. I have always had a quantitative bend anyway, and this surely seemed more interesting than sitting down and haggling all day between labor and management.

My interest was fostered by a successful summer job in the investment business in New York between the two years at the Business School. No doubt there is little better way to encourage interest in a particular field than through a summer job. I was fortunate in being hired to work in the research and investment advisory departments of White Weld & Co. in New York. My immediate supervisors were two great men—Frank Ritger and Thomas Pryor.

They were patient teachers and scholars in their own right, and they confirmed my impression that this was the field I should pursue. At first, it seemed just like HBS. My first assignment was writing letters to widows whose money was handled by the White Weld Investment Advisory Department. In the latter part of the summer I moved forward to the other extreme, banking and analysis of the fiber-glass boat business, which had just burst on the scene through forty or fifty small companies with some gel and a mold or two. This was at the other end of the speculative spectrum.

I came back from this summer encouraged by the variety of investment problems and by the brilliance of the associates. During the second year, my concentration was directed very closely to finance. Academic performance continued to be good and I was doing work that was directly related to what I thought my career would be.

Early in the second year, I began looking for a job in the investment business in Boston. Each of the large mutual funds would typically take one or two students from the Harvard Business School as would the banks and, perhaps, the insurance companies. Salaries were low, but advancement opportunities were supposedly great.

I was fortunate to be hired by a newly formed research department for F. S. Moseley & Co. The young research

THE ROLE OF INSTITUTIONS / 119

manager, who preceded me by less than a year, Robert F. A. Lawson, was an aggressive investor, oriented to magnificent operations in the exciting bull markets of the fifties. He was an excellent salesman and a sufficiently poor administrator to let me find my own way. Six months after I arrived, he left for a job with the legendary Gerald Tsai at Fidelity Fund, and I was put in charge of building our research department. Fortunately, no one else knew any more about what I should be doing than I did myself.

Qualities of an Investment Professional

The most highly prized characteristic of an investment professional is an ability to detach himself from his own self-interest. When one visits a doctor, he expects to be advised correctly whether he needs surgery, regardless of the financial outcome to the doctor. You want legal advice to avoid a court trial, even though it might oppose the best financial interests of the lawyer. An investment professional should be able to operate for his client, whether he be an investment manager or a broker, without excessive concern for his own self-interest. This is a rare characteristic and one to be hightly prized when found. It is frequently synonymous with integrity.

The old trustees of Boston had this quality in large measure. They were able to become a part of their client's problems and therefore could act as the client would himself, although from the standpoint of better knowledge about investment alternatives. Unfortunately, these traditions are dying out, and the new aggressiveness plus tougher business conditions within the investment community are making these old characteristics rare. They can still be found on whatever level of investment expertise may be required. The client should grasp and cherish them.

As the founder of a new investment counseling firm in 1969, I am partial to other firms that have recently started.

Those that have succeeded possess common characteristics that can be identified in other new firms: they have experienced people, they have a specific mission and, more important even than an established business base, they have a means of surviving, if only through their own savings, during the inherently difficult first several years. Some firms start on a marketing premise, and I think they fizzle out quickly. Others start to make an investment contribution and are apt to last and survive longer.

It is difficult when starting a new firm to assume that the founding fathers will be amicable. Investment people, as stated earlier, have large egos. They do not work well together, except by tremendous accommodation of their own personalities to the requirements of the organization or their security needs. It is for this reason that it is very desirable to start a new firm with people who have worked together, rather than just with those who think highly of themselves and may not respond well to the others.

One would expect institutional investors to be entrepreneurially oriented. Investment decisions are made frequently and on the basis of rather sketchy information. Those who are more methodical in their techniques would often be frustrated by their inability to obtain precisely the information that is proprietary to a particular company, but that also would be required to make a sound investment decision. To invest constantly with inadequate data would frustrate the more solid, scientific and often intellectual individual.

Despite the fact that successful investors share characteristics that might be damaging in other fields, investors are inherently conservative. Even when they throw their conservatism to the proverbial winds, they usually do so only when the consensus approach argues affirmatively. The late stages of a bull market, when the riskier and more highly leveraged securities are being bid up sharply in price, is the time when the most cautious investor tends to participate with the majority and follow the crowd.

The institutional investor is unhappy to be alone when the accuracy of his approach is not confirmed by his peers. He likes to see others who are similarly trained and similarly motivated doing the same things that he does at the same time. He often attempts to take a reading of the consensus and decides to join it.

It can be argued, however, that the consensus approach is unlikely to be profitable. Sensitivity to change is what investing is supposed to be about. Change presents opportunity as well as risk, particularly when it is appreciated by one investor before others. Change may take the form of an unfavorable surprise. It can also be the appreciation of an opportunity, which seems so obvious that it is difficult to see how it can be missed.

For example, after a decade of competing with cheaper goods from abroad, the United States textile industry is now in such a competitively strong position that we are and will likely continue to be net exporters to the world. The higher price for petroleum products will make small cars more economical and appealing to a larger segment of the market. Not only does this mean that fewer autos will be sold initially, but it accelerates the scrappage rate of older, less-economical vehicles and creates a better market for new units than would otherwise be the case.

The Third World now has money to accelerate its own industrial development from a greater proportion of the world's wealth going to raw materials suppliers. The Third World—what we used to call less-developed countries —wants food and technology, two products in which the United States is pre-eminent. We can provide them on the cheapest possible basis.

Although one would expect the investment professional to be sensitive to such changes, he has not been. So far in the early seventies he has been more sensitive to negative short-run changes that have plagued his own business, such as declining assets, disgruntled clients, and low trading volume. The investment community has resisted changes designed to lower the cost of services in order to attract more customers. It has balked against changes intended to accommodate the needs of more customers by combining the services now required by institutionally managed money, which may want brokerage and management services joined together.

Late in 1968, Keystone Funds considered establishing a separate account-management subsidiary. Keystone was one of the few mutual funds without a department that would manage pension, endowment funds, and the like. This was a logical extension of its investment-management capability, for it involved the further utilization of the research arm of the firm.

Mutual-fund sales had been poor. The last new funds introduced in the "go-go" days of 1967 sold well initially, but had performed so poorly that open-market sales were disappointing. Although I had some reservations and still do about the operational procedures of combining a registered investment advisory business with an investment company's business, it seemed a prudent step for Keystone.

There was general agreement among Keystone's management that such an activity should get under way. I was instrumental in examining the several alternatives for getting into this growing field. We had two options—the same as any new company—to be imitative, or innovative, and I was a strong but unsuccessful endorser of the innovative approach.

Keystone's investment activity is highly disciplined. It has funds of a defined-quality type, which must remain fully invested. It has the only fund division that can be designed to give the investment committee of sophisticated accounts an active hand in portfolio building. Most committees are frustrated when they delegate discretionary management to an investment manager. For one thing, they cannot tell whether they will get the product that they initially thought they should get. The manager they hire may change his mind. For another, they wonder if they will have any influence over investment decisions based upon their own opinion of the economic-market outlook.

The committee recognizes that they do not have access to the stock-selection information that will be required to make specific decisions. On the other hand, if one can operate on the Keystone system and produce a product of a defined-quality type, emphasizing only stock selection, the committee may—by taking various percentages of an account in S-1, 2, 3, 4, or some bond fund within the Keystone system—create a unique portfolio that will be responsive to the general business outlook of the committee and the stock-selection capability of Keystone.

Such a proposal would have also been an appropriate way to think of the fully managed fund at Keystone, known as K-2. It would have represented Keystone's answer as to how best to apportion the mix if one wished to rely upon Keystone for the overall portfolio balance. But it was particularly apt for the establishment of a new management company, because it would have been a new procedure that would have appealed to sophisticated accounts.

Another possible innovative approach was to combine all charges related to investment management into a single charge. Commissions may be a large and variable amount, which fluctuates according to the investment manager's desire for mobility. He obviously assumes this mobility, because he expects it to be more than compensated by results. But it seems logical to me that executions and mobility, like any other management cost, should be charged against the manager. He should have the incentive to reduce this charge and to test the level necessary to optimize the results. If any manager can operate more successfully with low transactions, he deserves to be rewarded with a higher profit margin. Correspondingly, the manager who requires a larger number of transactions to achieve his result should receive a lower profit margin.

I recommended that Keystone adopt a single fee and pay charges for brokerage out of the management fee, as well as absorb bank-custody costs. This procedure is often followed by investment-advisory departments associated with New York Stock Exchange brokers, where brokerage charges are credited against the management fee.

Keystone considered these options, together with a third option of establishing a conventional investment-management department with a sales-oriented individual, a single portfolio manager, and the very conventional approach of "doing the best job we know how." After all, Keystone had all of the research facilities of a large management company.

Characteristic of the conservative approach to business decisions made by the investment community, the decision to be imitative guaranteed that Keystone would not be embarrassed. Similarly, it reduced the chances of being highly successful to a very small figure.

Institutional Behavior

Institutional investors have risen steadily in importance throughout the post-World War II period. They dominate stock-market trading, are almost the sole investors in bonds, and, increasingly, have taken over control of venture-capital investment in private companies. Some institutional investors are required by law to be passive owners of corporations. Naturally, some have conduit tax treatment and few among them could seek to control companies even if they attempted to do so. The corporate role is essentially limited to selling a security when they are dissatisfied with the way a company is being run.

This abdication from the control function does not mean that institutions are not influential. Their attitudes are sought by companies; indeed, the institutions are courted. A merger between two companies is very difficult, if not impossible, to effect without the affirmative vote of institutions representing both parties.

Institutions are wooed by companies because their buying interest benefits security prices. A security with an institutional following usually sells higher on average than comparable issues without institutional sponsorship. The cost of equity capital thus becomes cheaper and an institutional following facilitates the company's financial planning.

Institutional sponsorship obviously increases the volatility of a stock, for institutions tend to move in or out with market orders. The number of institutionally dumped securities is greater each year and is compounded by the fact that when one or two institutions decide to sell a stock the other institutions, fearing that a down-trend may develop, may actually create the trend by joining the selling movement.

Institutions have no hocus-pocus method of investing funds more profitably than anyone else. The publication of performance results is more common for mutual funds than for other types of institutions; indeed, they may be typical of a group of institutional investors as a whole. There is little evidence that mutual funds have done better in the aggregate than an individual might achieve by selecting securities at random from a particular risk level. By extension, these data imply that similar results would be obtained by banks, insurance companies, and large private investors with a staff of investment people working for them.

Institutional investors tend to be faddists. They are very concerned about what will be bought or sold by other

institutions in the next year or two, and they are more interested in practicing successfully the "greater fool" theory
than in making fundamental determinations of value. After
all, values may be undiscovered for a long time, whereas the
discovery of an industry itself can bring quick profit.

In the last decade, I have observed at least four substantial booms in housing-related securities, without the
benefit of a housing boom. We still have that to anticipate.
One sometimes forgets that institutions are the same as any
other organization. There are internal politics; success does
not correlate always with skill; and there are the normal or-
ganizational strains and jealousies, most of which hamper
communications.

Organizations have become more tightly structured
recently, primarily to protect members from criticism. This
is fashioned after the old guilds; it prevents members from
being picked off, one by one, for inferior work.

The amount of paper moving through institutions
today is at least double that of two years ago, but I doubt if
it reflects an improved quality of work. Although institutions
are designed to provide a professional service, they are run
by people with a sales background. Consequently, marketing
usually receives considerable emphasis.

Keystone Funds is a good sample institution. In my
three years there, I held a number of jobs: analyst, associate
director of research, director of research, portfolio manager.
Keystone was founded during the thirties, when many successful funds began. Any firm that survived the difficult Depression and World War II years had a good chance of pros-
pering during the two decades of boom that followed.

The fund's strong first-generation management died,
or retired, and was succeeded by a second generation of employees, rather than by entrepreneurs. The Keystone spread
of funds was unique. But it never capitalized upon this attri-
bute, due to fears that it would appear less involved with

the consensus than was actually the case. It has stressed conventional methods of marketing, and its newer funds have been conventional "me-too" products rather than the progressive investment vehicles that built the organization initially.

The Keystone investment systems were designed to be run by automatons. In fact, they were set up by a salesman so that he could control the investment process without having to hire expensive talent. In recent years Keystone has competed with conventional institutional investment talent and has run into problems trying to get creative people to adapt to an externally imposed system. The result has been a poor marriage of the two, an unspectacular result from persons misfitted to the product.

Two challenges have been presented to institutions in the last ten years. The first challenge came from academics in the mid sixties who processed huge amounts of stock-market data and concluded that institutional results were not the result of skillful professional selection but of chance. Furthermore, they concluded that the good institutions, as demonstrated by past records, had no greater chance to continue to be good institutions in the future than those that had been demonstrably poor. Rather than accepting this challenge, and adapting to it or refuting the figures, the institutions ignored the challenge. Currently, the institutions are suffering from this behavior because individual investors have been voting with their feet (by steadily redeeming their mutual-fund holdings) and because they have been reluctant to give other professional investors their money to manage.

Institutions themselves are now beginning to accept the academic notion without controversy. The same institutions that ignored the academic challenge earlier are now willing to accept it without attempting to find cases where they can make a professional contribution. They are willing to adapt their organizations around the idea that if they are going to achieve chance results, they should do everything possible to insure that they rest in the middle of the pack, rather than at the extremes of the distribution. They will rely upon sales techniques to achieve their business ends.

The second challenge has been steady pressure from government sources. Here, most institutions have fought with their own trade associations in an attempt to stop government regulation of their business. I think the institutions are correct in assuming that government regulations tend to solve last year's problems and create an unnecessary burden on a continuing basis.

Political campaigns have been financed and pressure has been brought to bear on legislators. Preserving self-regulation in the institutions themselves is a losing battle. A few institutional leaders have taken constructive steps to educate regulators in the way in which securities markets operate, but they have been rare.

I have not seen, for example, any type of intern or executive-exchange program between government regulators and institutions. One would expect that the benefits to be received from such a program could be immense. Instead, an air of hostility and suspicion exists, which thwarts almost any constructive policy.

It seems to me that the sole function of an institution is to provide a professional service that individuals or companies cannot supply for themselves. The function of an institution is not to provide a means of livelihood for its employees. If one accepts my objective, institutions should strive to be innovative; otherwise, the clients would soon learn to emulate the institutions. Yet innovation may be risky for an institution's employees. By being innovative, you increase the chance of being wrong as you are in unexplored territory.

Newer firms tend to have more satisfied clients because they have been founded on the principle of satisfying clients' needs. Furthermore, they must be run without the expenditure of great marketing effort and talent. The professional service concentration of the newer firm is proportionately higher in most cases than of the older firm that is dedicated to the preservation of its employees' base of livelihood.

The fact is that employees of institutions are characterized by their age, far more than by the type of institution they may be working for. The senior officers now are mostly former professional managers or salesmen who entered the investment field in the late forties or early fifties. It was not a choice industry at that time and not very many people were coming in. The investment business did not get first crack at the best brains. Those who have risen to a leadership postition did so as much by being there at the right time as by their own wit. The earlier innovators and entrepreneurs who started the firms in the thirties have nearly all retired or died. In any event, they have lost their influence.

The equivalent of a middle-management group—department heads and the like—joined institutions during the late fifties to mid sixties. As a group, they are perhaps brighter and more aggressive than seniors. They entered the investment business believing that it was the fastest way to succeed financially. Most institutions have provided a somewhat disillusioning environment for these individuals who probably rose quickly through the junior positions. But throughout most of the recent time in which they have held senior responsibility, the institutions have been on the defensive with their clients and in a state of turmoil. These men did not expect to be engaged in a rearguard action. They were trained for exploiting bull markets.

This group is most disillusioned and harbors severe internal strains. On the one hand, livelihoods are threatened by life styles that require fairly large salaries. On the other hand, their particular work is not satisfying and growth requirements are not being met.

The third group—analysts, portfolio managers, computer people—is the happiest. Young people who have entered institutions in the last several years, like their top company officers, are not the pick of the crop. They were trained at business schools and were told that it's all a marketing business anyway.

The most-skilled marketing people gravitate more toward Procter & Gamble than toward Morgan Guaranty. Those who did go into the investment business had low expectations—the immediate salaries were good, but career aspirations were modest. They are security conscious and find that the institutional world suits their preconceptions; that is, if they just put in their time they will advance at a normal pace.

These three groups find it very difficult to communicate with one another. At least half of their effort is spent in establishing communications channels. The healthy breakout of intensive competition is almost always missing. The competition is most destructive. There is no easy way to cure these problems, but in many institutions they're not even recognized.

Institutional investors like to combine business and social affairs. After all, it is much better to conduct business over cocktails or a meal—essentially disarming social occasions. Small talk is more acceptable and the guest is under more obligation to listen to any proposal the host may discuss. Moreover, this practice allows one to extend his day from breakfast through dinner if required.

One of the more interesting social-cum-business affairs was arranged recently for a small group of investment leaders by a New York broker, who offered to introduce investors to a small group of European banking houses. This broker is also an investment-management firm that has a slight working relationship with European investment management and brokerage firms. A high-level friendship with a European banking firm is at least as important as technical confidence in maintaining good working relationships. Firms in Europe tend to exchange junior employees, so that working relationships are built up over a lifetime among them.

This broker has a tradition of being the U.S. arm of its European associates and is responsible for investing some U.S. dollars for the group members. He could offer the services of the European group to a small number of American institutions. This is a traditional way of servicing investors by arranging introductions.

I accepted an invitation to visit several countries on a European trip and spent several days in each country seeing government officials, company managements, and bankers under the auspices of the banking firm in each country. One of the more illuminating sessions, which best describes how a social affair establishes a business relationship, was lunch at the Rothschild bank in Paris.

The Rothschilds had just built a new building several blocks from the Bourse. It was the only building in Paris I noticed without a street number on the facade. Clearly, it was the most imposing building in the area. I learned later that it had been built on the site of the original Rothschild bank, the construction taking place while the Rothschild banking offices were headquartered temporarily across the street. The tradition of being on the same geographical spot as the original bank was important enough to justify this additional expense.

The program of the day consisted of a reception, followed by lunch on the top floor, and briefings at the Bourse that were arranged by the Rothschild officers. I arrived slightly early for lunch. My own business needed attention that morning, and I did not stay with the group.

A white-gloved, tail-coated usher directed me into a panoramic cocktail room overlooking Montmartre with the Basilica of Sacré-Coeur a mile away, but almost at eye level. We stood around for a while and I was offered a drink by yet another servant, a cocktail which a third butler served on a silver tray. Within a few minutes the Baron Guy de Rothschild appeared with a portion of his younger coterie in tow.

As nearly as I could tell, there were at least three hosts at each table; one senior gentleman, who guided the conversation and pleasantries, one of the young members of the Rothschild international department, and one miscellaneous official.

I was seated at a table with Baron Philippe de Rothschild, who reputedly is the style-setter for European fashions. Much of our conversation concerned the prices of wine and the desirability that such prices decline. My suggestion that California whites can be improved by adding CO_2 in a seltzer maker brought a look of anguish on Baron de Rothschild's face. I described it as "goosing" the wine. I suspect that I provided him with an "Ugly American" story for years to come.

No business was discussed during luncheon. As soon as it was over, Guy de Rothschild made a short speech in which he touched lightly upon the views of the bank and conditions around the world. France was in good shape although inflation was increasing. Germany looked all right, but the rise of socialism should be bad for investment. Britain was like a poor aunt; Italy an errant child. Switzerland was not discussed, but I suspect it might have passed his test in the number-two spot after France.

I noticed that here and in other banking institutions there are two levels of management. Each group had a half-dozen or so young technocrats, graduates of École Politechnique, or an American business school, fluent in English and conversant with American institutional-investment terminology. These go-getters would seek out their guests and could have conversed with any American broker about European investment opportunities.

On the other hand, each firm had an older group that did not go out of its way to speak English, or, in fact, did not listen to the presentations of its own younger group. Perhaps I am overgeneralizing, but I have the strong impression that the older group represents the power center in each of the banks, whereas the others are merely senior employees.

The decision to do business with an American firm may involve far more personal judgment on the part of senior management than the rational assessment of business opportunities provided by the juniors.

After lunch we walked down the street to the stock exchange and entered a small amphitheater on the second floor. Here we sat in overstuffed theater chairs to view a twenty-minute film on the operation of the Paris Bourse. After a two-and-a-half-hour lunch and three wines, no one was awake when the lights were turned on again. It was especially courteous of our hosts to think of arranging an opportunity for the traditional European "siesta."

In an investment partnership, which so often must take place as one internationalizes a portfolio, class is important. Although there is a tendency to think of class-consciousness within the investment field as snobbery (and it may be), if one is going to turn over sums of money to another banking house in another country with an entirely different set of rules and to another person, predictability of behavior is critical. Individuals who have gone to school together, worked together as juniors, and played and socialized together are likely to be far more predictable than those who have developed only a recent commercial relationship.

In the continual discussion among institutions as to

who is friendly with whom, friendship becomes in effect their technique of determining predictability. In every country visited it was *de rigueur* to attend a lavish banquet at night (if not also at noon). Each member consequently suffered from traveler's indigestion. We soon developed a bond of sympathy that was founded upon the necessity of frequent and sudden departures from the meeting room.

As a result of banquets night after night, I now have a first-hand understanding of the problems of people in the diplomatic corps. As I said in a toast in Germany: "Napoleon's army is not the only group to have traveled on its stomach!"

The cleavage between institutionalized and noninstitutionalized securities is much sharper in Europe than in the United States. Because the markets are thinner and the commercial base narrower, each European country has only a few major capitalized companies that can be internationally owned. These sell at triple or quadruple the prices of the smaller companies, which are essentially owned in the domestic markets.

We visited several of the major companies in each country—Sieman's in Germany, Phillips in Holland, and others. Presentations at these companies were facsimiles of their American counterparts: a briefing by officials in the equivalent of the planning department, a luncheon, and, quite likely, a product demonstration.

I left with the impression that each company felt that conditions in its own country were not very good, but that expansion opportunities in all the other countries were excellent. In other words, the European company saw only limited opportunities in its traditional markets but expected to be able to move into somebody else's market. On an overall basis, this expression did not augur well for the likelihood of success.

For the first time, in Europe I was exposed to what

may later come in the United States, that is, the companies there were earning only 4 or 5 percent on their invested capital, but they were expanding capacity while borrowing money at 10 to 15 percent because construction costs were rising at 20 percent per year. If they did not expand now, the expansion would be much more expensive later due to inflation.

7

The Investment Firm

Mutual-fund organizations are strange beasts. The management companies themselves have sponsored funds in order to establish assets that these sponsoring organizations can manage. However, the funds themselves are under the direct responsiblity of independent directors. They are chosen by the sponsoring organization but, ostensibly, represent the interests of the fund's shareholders even where they may differ from that of the sponsor. In theory, investment decisions and policies must be controlled by independent directors, although in practice they are mere rubber stamps of the management company.

On many occasions, I have attended meetings with a sponsor's independent directors. The format is almost always identical—a review of performance, restatement of objectives, investment outlook, and questions. The questions are usually polite (but during the poor-performance period of many mutual-fund organizations, they are getting harsher). The questions characteristically involve looking down the portfolio list to see what was sold at a great loss and asking about safeguards to prevent such a blunder from recurring. Or, the portfolio will be examined for sources of unrealized capital losses and the portfolio manager will be asked why he is staying with such "dogs" when he could have bought more of the stocks in the portfolio that went up.

The independent director's motives are in part financial; they are often well paid for this responsibility, although there is a question as to whether the pay is sufficient for the legal liability they may be assuming or for the prestige and information. A directorship involves, in most cases, spending a day probing around and getting the best thinking of an investment organization. Yet at no time does the system really serve the interests of the fund's shareholders. One characteristic is that there has been only one occasion to my knowledge when the independent directors of a mutual fund have actually shifted the management contract from one sponsoring organization to another.

Investment organizations of all types have a very horizontal structure. They have not had, until recently, several management layers. Instead, they have operated more like a university with independent faculties and a dean, whose task it is to provide a fully functioning environment and the services necessary to support specialized faculties. The investment function is an intense emotional experience and one that would logically require rotation through different types of portfolios or into other parts of the business to maintain a freshness of spirit. Rotation usually takes place only when failure has been achieved.

In fact, one difficulty of large investment organizations is an inability to shift people to different functions. To be sure, portfolio managers may be transferred from one type of account to another—from a yield to an appreciation account, for example—or moved into the bond area.

But rarely does this take place with corporate functions. Oc-cupational rotation is done as a normal course for training the broad-gauged business executive. Rarely in an invest-ment organization are there any transfers among the three aspects of the firm—administration, marketing, investment.

All investment organizations have very high operating leverage, although the apparent nature of the business is volatile, depending upon changes in market value. Fees are computed upon asset value or on brokerage charges for transactions, both of which tend to rise during periods of good markets and contract during poor markets. Most costs are fixed and do not vary with transactions. So profits are high during prosperous market periods, which encourages firms to expand at a time when they should be holding fast, and profits are low during depressed market periods. This is a service business with little need for fixed capital, except for preparing for poor years to come. The financial reserves for unfavorable years for brokers and institutions tend to be relatively small. Overall, the returns on capital for long pe-riods of time tend to be exceptionally generous.

With the substantial operating leverage in this busi-ness, it would seem very odd to add financial leverage on top. On the other hand, brokers characteristically borrow a great deal of money and produce the worst possible combi-nation of operating and financial leverage. This combina-tion is perhaps one reason why brokers, as the spearhead of the investment business, experienced serious financial re-verses in the early seventies.

Most large investment firms spend much of their time communicating. Decision-making is diffused among a variety of portfolio managers, analysts, and staff advisors, such as economists and traders. A single decision is often made by all of these levels working together, communicating the essential information required to make such decisions. Ego-involvement in any portfolio decision-making is quite high. At each level are highly skilled and trained individuals. Much of the effort of the organization must be spent in facilitating the communications flow. It is well known that a squad-sized group of eight to ten can operate quite informally but, beyond that number, status, strata, and formality take over. Morning meetings are essential for informing a large number of people about what is going on within the organization. The paperwork flow must be analyzed, with snap-out carbon forms going to individuals who may not be directly involved in the line of a decision-making process, but who must be kept informed in the event that they have to step into the process in an emergency.

Most large investment firms seem to spend most of their time communicating and very little in thinking or decision-making. Perhaps this is another reason why large investment organizations are loathe to make investment decisions. These monoliths believe in holding a portfolio that will behave in line with market expectations, while at the same time they pay ceremonial or religious lip service to practices of investment analysis or portfolio management that in the distant past have produced success.

In the most diffused investment institutions it is somewhat more difficult to determine precisely when an investment decision is reached and by whom. There has been a full swing away from the superstar days of the sixties to the market-portfolio days a decade later. Now, few decisions are made, objectives are modest, and a slow pace, organizationally, is followed. A defensive posture is demanded. This is a 180-degree turn from the mid sixties, when striving for top place on anybody's performance list was the objective, and some took the extraordinary risk of placing huge assets into the potentially capricious hands of lone, untrained individuals.

I can speculate that ten years from now entire areas of the so-called middle management of investment firms will be replaced by quantitative operational tools with the principal decision-making being done by a few top-level people.

A great deal of the business of the investment community is conducted over lunch, which may be the most important session of the day. A luncheon meeting will typically last an hour and a half to two hours and may include a formal presentation. Lunch is usually structured around one or more persons trying to persuade other individuals of another company or department to adopt the views of the first group.

One of the more common luncheon settings is a bank. Some of the more select private banks, or large investment banking houses, maintain excellent dining rooms for entertaining clients. Here the topics are more general, the evidence of papers at the table is considered gauche, and the menus will surpass even the finest restaurants in the city. Lunch will nearly always be followed by coffee and cigars where more specific "buttonholing" takes place if required. Boston is less noted for private dining rooms than New York, but the city has several first-class competitors in the race for culinary excellence. Brown Brothers, Harriman has long held the top spot, although a newcomer, Alliance Capital, a division of Donaldson, Lufkin & Jenrette, is competing for a five-star rating.

The message the host conveys to his guest is severalfold. He is saying that the elaborately prepared and served luncheon is the way the host lives all the time. Working with him—thereby hiring the host to manage the guest's worldly goods—naturally insures that the guest too will live similarly well. Few guests react negatively. They seldom recognize that the host is allocating his resources to a chef, rather than hiring one more senior analyst.

Under some conditions, the public display of ostentation has backfired. The typical old Boston trustee will maintain an office in dingy, dusty quarters and drive home in a rattly old Ford, while controlling assets of hundreds of millions of dollars. No client visiting him in his office surroundings would feel as though the fees were being misapplied, whether or not such was the case.

Keystone built an elaborate building at a time when mutual funds were under attack for having excessive fees relative to the performance and satisfaction received by its clients. Atop the building, it put its trademark, advertising to the world that it had enough money to pay for real estate, but did not have enough at the present fee structure to hire additional people to improve the results of assets under its care.

Brokers have been especially susceptible to the idea that clients will associate elaborate office quarters with success and that this will be a marketing aid. The expensive offices and leasehold improvements acquired by brokers in the last ten years may be more responsible for their demise than any other single force. An old-line, respected, well-capitalized firm—Clark, Dodge—built the most elaborate brokerage office space in Boston in the tower of the new First National Bank building. For two years the office was less than half filled. The firm was unable to acquire new salesmen to fill these opulent surroundings. Whether the clients reacted negatively to the surroundings, I don't know. It is more than coincidental that Clark, Dodge was recently taken over on knockdown bargain terms by Kidder Peabody, which maintains crowded offices in an old building.

The broker or investment manager who thinks that lavish surroundings and luncheons are conducive to a professional relationship should be reminded again of the expression: "Where are the customers' yachts?"

Selecting an Investment Firm

Individuals and tax-free institutions seek investment managers in a different format, although their fundamental reasons may be the same. They want to trust the people they select and they expect efficiency. That is, they want higher returns than average at an acceptable level of risk.

The first clients of most new firms are individual investors, as opposed to institutions. They usually are not very sophisticated about investment techniques but are accustomed to judge professionals by the look in their eye, the manner and sincerity of their approach to the client's problems, and by matching their own personality against the professional. The client wants a professional investment manager who will behave as the client would himself if he had access to the same information.

The decision-making process is relatively swift. The unsophisticated individual does not enjoy talking with many professional investors. He frequently does not know what specific questions to ask, but he does know that his decision will be based upon factors other than those that may relate to the investment activities of the professional.

Credentials are important; they at least give evidence that original skills are present. But more directly, one has a feeling that the decision is made quickly in an interview session and on the basis of intuition far more than from an objective check list. The early clients of our new firm tended to be individual investors and, since even our smallest accounts were quite large, they obviously were people of wealth.

Few individuals open an account with a relatively new firm for their first investment-management experience. We saw investors who were on the rebound from other investment activities.

These investors were of two types: individuals who had been with banks who, because of the size of their account in comparison to the large trusts, found they were being shuffled frequently between junior trust officers; and secondly, individuals with engineering or scientific backgrounds who thought perhaps that our investment approach was more quantitatively oriented and less mystical than others.

The typical individual is directed to a new firm by a friend or sometimes a broker. The recent investment record of the prospective manager is important. Few investors can make the act of faith required to choose a new investment manager whose record has been poor. Several visits may be involved; in fact, they are desired.

The initial visit establishes the base. The interval between the preliminary and the concluding session gives the individual time to think of new questions and to assign in his own mind a priority of the strengths and weaknesses of the investment firm he is considering.

The format for large tax-free institutions has evolved into a set pattern. These institutions are accustomed to splitting their funds among as many as twenty, but more likely half a dozen, investment managers. The early form of splitting was based upon the notion that competitive assignments of assets would produce better investment results, and the account would be split initially into approximately equal parts.

Subsequent experience has disproved this competitive-capital approach. We have discovered that the investment manager cannot escape from his specific investment-strategy mold, even if he tries. The sense of competition of variance in fee schedules makes little difference to the results that will be achieved by any one client versus another. Accounts now are attempting to split, in order to diversify investment styles and strategies and to pick the manager best suited for a particular investment approach. It is hoped that, by blending the best of high-yield, high-value, fad, or institutionally acceptable securities, one can get diversification and better results. Each style is expected to have some selection ability within its defined strategy, with a result that will produce better figures than a purely random sample drawn from each of the defined styles.

Initial lists comprising as many as a hundred potential candidates will be drawn from the reputations and hearsay as to which is doing a good job. A search committee will be formed that can be the same as a pension committee in a large company, or a finance committee for an eleemosynary institution. It is customary to send questionnaires to prospective candidates, designed to illuminate the differences among firms. Questionnaires are usually a dozen pages in length when completed but they include mostly the same questions.

Batterymarch receives several dozen questionnaires a year from large pools of money searching for investment managers. The questions are almost always the same: how large are you, how many accounts do you have, how are you organized, how do you reach investment decisions, what is your performance and so on.

Most such questions get relatively standard answers from us and other respondents. They do little to define the principal differences among firms, but merely provide a factual basis for confirming decisions that have already been made to accept or reject.

An exception to the rule of preordained decisions was one widely circulated questionnaire by the newly formed Harvard Management Company in its quest for outside managers in 1974. It illuminates factors one institutional investor considers significant about another. The questions they asked are as follows: *

---

* Reprinted with permission of Harvard Management Company, Boston, Massachusetts.

COMPANY BACKGROUND AND OPERATIONS

1. Name of company
2. Year organized
3. Ownership
4. Affiliated companies and relationship
5. Number of accounts with full discretion by size and type currently managed by your firm:

   What was the number of new accounts acquired in each of the years 1972 and 973 and their asset value?

   What was the number of accounts lost in each of the years 1972 and 1973 and their asset value?

   What is your firm's minimum-size account
   a. With positive cash flow?
   b. With no cash flow?

   Does your firm manage any mutual funds?
6. Management fee schedule. Please describe any exceptions.

INVESTMENT PHILOSOPHY AND POLICY

1. As we are looking for a number of complementary philosophies among our managers rather than a single philosophy, it would be helpful if you could outline your organization's investment philosophy in some detail, including sample portfolios from the past two years to illustrate your approach. Please indicate how your philosophy may have changed over the past five years.
2. In addition, it would be helpful to us if you could comment on such investment policy questions as your attitude toward using market cycles, your time horizon in making investments and taking profits, what size company capitalizations you are most comfortable with, your

principles of portfolio diversification, and your historical and expected portfolio turnover rates.

ORGANIZATION

1. A. Please indicate the number of full-time portfolio man-
        agers in your organization and include resumes if
        available.
    B. Please indicate the number of full-time analysts, ex-
        cluding clerical assistants, and include resumes if
        available.
2. Please attach an organization chart if appropriate, indi-
    cating flow of information and authority with names of
    individuals.
3. Please indicate what additions and subtractions of pro
    fessional personnel have occurred over the past two years.
4. Please indicate how much of the typical portfolio man-
    ager's and analyst's time is spent on marketing and ad-
    ministration functions.
5. Please indicate the portfolio manager or managers who
    would be responsible for the management of a portion of
    Harvard's assets. Please also outline his or her other cur-
    rent and projected responsibilities in your firm, includ-
    ing marketing, administration, and the management of
    other portfolios.
6. Is there any firm policy that would prevent your firm
    from working closely in a complementary relationship
    with Harvard's internal management company?
7. Please indicate what the overall objectives of your firm
    are with respect to your future growth in general, and
    comment particularly on any present or planned areas of
    your business that you expect will be emphasized in the
    future.

RESEARCH AND THE DECISION MAKING PROCESS

1. Please describe the process by which an investment idea
    is originated, researched, evaluated, and ultimately be-

comes an investment decision. In particular, with respect to portfolio managers, please indicate what is the optimum number of accounts for each manager and what individual discretion with respect to overall philosophy or individual stocks he or she has in structuring portfolios with comparable objectives.

2. A. With respect to research, we are interested in knowing your sources of information and ideas about the general direction of the economy and market, the relative attractiveness of different industries and companies, and the relative emphasis that you place on fundamental or technical analysis. In addition we would like to know whether, and, if so, how, you attempt to quantify your estimates of potential rate of return; how you measure risk in choosing an individual security and structuring your portfolio; and what techniques of control and evaluation you employ to monitor your present and prospective holdings for buy and sell decision.

   B. How big is the investment universe you monitor for possible new holdings and how many companies do you generate earnings estimates for internally.

   C. What other techniques do you employ to develop or check investment ideas, which are not outlined in the questions above.

PERFORMANCE DATA

Annual change in per share (unit) at the beginning of the year for (a) all growth or balanced accounts under management, or (b) several typical growth or balanced accounts, preferably $10 million or larger, or (c) a public record growth or balanced account such as mutual funds or common trust funds. If you are able to supply (a), (b), and (c), please do so and note which performance is being supplied.

The questions can be summarized: who, what, where, how, how much? The results among the larger firms are not dispersed widely, as are those of smaller firms. Expenses can range from nothing, for someone who wants to make a price concession in order to get a lead account, to charges of one or two percent of market value.

The answers are usually amplifications of material that may have been published in brochures. But they can go into far more detail, since the brochures go through extensive legal clearance, and must necessarily be more general in order to remain up to date for several years.

The prospective candidate usually plagiarizes answers for other recent searches of large accounts. Following receipt of the questionnaire, the prospective large account reviews the material, usually with an idea of establishing the best candidate in each of the investment styles he wishes to hire.

It is not uncommon for a group to sit around a table and sort out the questionnaires in the order of their merit. This stage often determines the ultimate decision. On the basis of the written material and the record and defined style of an investment manager, the committee members can gauge quite well their ultimate choice. But the most intense individual activity is still to come.

Invitations for presentation, usually an hour in length, are sent to a selection of candidates. This session is usually referred to as the "semifinals." A team of representatives from the prospective firm are invited to the institution's offices to make a presentation, which is not unlike the preliminary presentation that advertising firms make to prospective clients.

It usually involves a two- or three-man group, perhaps a senior investment-company official, a marketing-oriented individual, and an individual who might be personally in charge of the account in question. The presentation will be to a committee of the tax-free institution and is an attempt by both parties to see how the personalities fit.

The presentation is usually opened by the marketing representative who gives the firm's history, the business objectives, and the types of people involved at the investment institution. The senior investment officer describes how investment decisions are reached and perhaps reviews the current economic and investment outlook.

The prospective portfolio manager then describes how he would handle the transition of the new account were he assigned to the task. The normal cut within a one-hour presentation would be thirty to forty minutes of formal briefing, followed by questions for the remainder of the hour. As many as six presentations could take place in one day. I often have the impression that they added little to the decision-making process, except that some firms, which had previously been considered to be high candidates, do not show up as well face to face as they do on the written material.

Of the twenty or so candidates making the formal presentation in the semifinals, perhaps eight or ten will be dropped. The remaining candidates will be visited by one or two members of the search committee at the home offices of the institutions under consideration. Of the final candidates, usually one out of two will be selected.

The process from beginning to end typically averages a year and involves an expenditure of man-hours by client and investment institution that easily exceeds one hundred thousand dollars. Some clients hire consultants to assist them with the initial screening, determination of objectives, and fact gathering. As in most fields, consultants who engage in this work have skills that range from zero to superior.

One of the hallmarks of a true professional is the ease with which he conducts his affairs. He gives no sign of strain, although his output is greater than most others. He gives the impression of having ample reserve power to call upon in an emergency, but, never having to face an emergency, he can easily handle any problems that arise.

One portfolio manager at Keystone was responsible for his fund for over ten years. I never knew his educational background, but I suspected it did not include an advanced degree. Moreover, he was ten or fifteen years older than the graduate-school-trained portfolio managers who were taking hold. He had no great quantitative skills, and tended to work only half a day. His lunch was not a discussion of business problems, but was more likely consumed with one or two cronies from the firm at some no-name restaurant where the principal feature was inexpensive martinis served in a water glass.

Afternoons were not productive for this portfolio manager. If he didn't make a decision by noon, he had sense enough to know that he should not make it in his afternoon condition. When the new group of scientific managers took over, this portfolio manager looked completely out of place. Regardless of his fund's record, he was unable to explain why he was making certain decisions and made the process look as though he didn't care. It was embarrassing that he worked only half the time and one could be concerned that he would undermine the morale of the younger men.

For reasons of technique, far more than result, the responsibility for his fund was transferred and he moved to another organization. In time, I began to realize that he was one of the most professional portfolio managers I knew. He had a universe of two hundred and fifty securities from which he had to choose eighty for his fund. His task, he felt, was to eliminate the hundred and seventy he didn't want to buy. From an operational sense, this didn't require full-time decision-making, and he didn't feel up-tight about his job. He was quite relaxed, but it just did not look right in the demanding period of the sixties.

Another man who seemed misplaced was a mutual-fund technician. He might have had a high-school education, but I'm not sure. His entire approach to the market was completely mechanical. He used the rule of three, which said that if you took measuring calipers and spaced off distances on a chart (I was never sure if he used an arithmetic or geometric grid), you could forecast price targets for individual securities and market trends.

For some years he had been running mechanically selected portfolios, comparable to the Keystone portfolios. His mechanical hypothetical portfolios invariably outperformed the real accounts, although one could hardly ever understand why. It seemed to smack of examining the rooster's entrails in the morning at the temple but it worked. He never seemed to experience the same indecision about the future that plagued the rest of us. He could examine his scrolls and tell exactly where we were. No one used his technical service and eventually he retired.

Client/Investment Firm Communications

Some clients have no desire to talk to their investment manager. Once they have delegated the responsibility, they prefer to have no further thought about it, especially when it is painful. With these clients, under adverse conditions, manager and client behave in exactly the same way; they have no contact until things get better and conversations can be more pleasant. It is our normal practice to communicate with clients on a monthly or quarterly basis. We have a church group that said it wanted only to be informed of the investment situation every five years. I assume that they are looking into their investment performance over a very long time, once every generation. We have, in this case, communicated quarterly.

Other clients want frequent discussions with their investment manager, i.e., weekly calls, discussions about the impact of specific events on market prices, and general attention to short-term information. I have seen no indication that such a stress on short-term communications is productive for anyone. It is the type of communication that many individual clients are accustomed to having with their broker, and it relates far more to a trading philosophy than to an investment-management activity.

When times are good an investment manager is frequently inclined to write his client and say "the numbers speak for themselves." But writing that type of letter is risky in a bad quarter, for the client may return a copy with a postscript added: "Send me my funds."

There seems to be an inverse relationship between the length of an investment manager's letter to his client and market performance. When conditions are poor, the manager has to go to greater lengths to point out that some of the loss was due to bad luck, that the part that was due to poor skills had been corrected. When good results stem from generally favorable market conditions, few managers feel compelled to write long explanations about the mistakes that were made that did not show up because the rising market itself bailed out the error.

I have extracted portions from client letters to illustrate the tone that is taken after different market performances. The letter covers the general outlook for the economy and the market, a review of past results, and a forecast for the future with an outline of what sort of portfolio action is likely in the next quarter.

The letters were written to sophisticated individual clients:

Date: April 1974   Good Results

". . . In terms of comparative market performance, this quarter was very satisfactory. . . .

"We have continued to emphasize defensive earnings. Government economic figures suggest the recession began in

November 1973. The recession is likely to measure between average and mild, perhaps not dissimilar from the 1969–70 period. It will be characterized, however, by sharp differences in results with some industries operating under boom conditions and others under stringency. Profit levels for the year may be higher than our original forecast of flat to down slightly. Price levels in the industrial sector are rising fast enough to absorb the slippage in unit costs and small gains of volume. The industrial raw material price increase of over 60 percent worldwide last year should steadily moderate its rate of gain as the year continues. . . .

"You will be interested to know that the average earnings per share gain of your portfolio approximated 20 percent. More importantly, we have selected companies during the past year for their characteristics to do well in a recessionary year. Although we might expect mild gains in corporate profits in 1974, our current forecast is that your portfolio earnings gains will be five percentage points higher. We believe this difference as well as the higher-than-average yield should make these companies comparative standouts as the year progresses. . . ."

Date: April 1972   Good Results and Preparation
for Poor Market

"Your account stands at nearly $4.5 million at the close of the quarter, a reasonable milestone since we started at just slightly over $3 million in the middle of 1970. In percentage terms, the results have been greater adjusting for the account withdrawals. The percentage increase of 10 percent versus some 5 percent in the Standard & Poor's 500 Index would not have been possible in the first quarter except in a favorable environment. We have, however, been reasonably risk-conscious throughout the period and the resistance of the portfolio in earlier down market periods suggests that we may do reasonably well if the market declines now.

"Approximately one quarter of the portfolio was sold and reinvested in securities that serve a "two-hat" function —securities that will likely do better than the market whether up or down. The sales were made principally on those items that had, on average, a 50 percent profit where we no longer considered the securities to be unusually good values. . . .

"By any historic measures, the market is high. The yield spread between the Standard & Poor's 500 Index and long-term bonds is almost five percentage points, the market has become progressively more speculative during the quarter, and it is more difficult for us to find security ideas at a reasonable price which appears as attractive to us as opportunities were during 1971. We are responding to these conditions by reducing the cyclical exposure to less than half of the portfolio and looking for opportunities to increase more defensive areas like regional banks and life insurance, where opportunities exist to satisfy our growth and earnings-mulitiple criteria. We have no plans to carry a large cash position but do plan to adhere rigorously to our practice of taking profits wherever they occur. Essentially we have done better in a rising market than I would have forecasted, and we are currently trying to build into the portfolio characteristics that protect these gains. I have no clear market forecast but have a hunch that the end of the year may be softer than the early part of the year."

Date: July 1973   Explaining Poor Results

". . . This seeming lack of resistiveness to a generally used market index has surprised us and precipitated a re-examination of our strategy. I know you will be interested in the results since we were attempting to answer the question on what modifications, if any, we should make in our basic investment approach.

"The average decline of all New York Stock Exchange stocks for the first half has been just over 30 percent this year, and your account has declined by 20.8 percent. Painful for us is the relative success of the Standard & Poor's 500, off only 11 percent. We have found, the hard way, that one cannot tie short-term performance to the S&P 500. It has become so weighted by growth stocks that it behaves like a growth-stock index, increasingly independent of the mass of stocks.

"Fortunately, our selectivity against the mass of stocks has remained. For all accounts, our lead over the average move of all NYSE stocks has been:

1970　+11.9%　　1971　+7.1%　　1972　+9.1%
Six months 1973　+12% annual rate

"Investment gains from this level could be unusually high. The ratio of the mass of stocks to the senior 100 has always reversed from similar depressed levels. From current overselling due to loss of confidence, multiples could recover over the next few years in the range of +10 percent to +40 percent. Probable exceptions would be most of the growth stocks currently at peak multiples. Present portfolio yield of 5 percent is itself a good return. Real growth of the economy is likely to remain slightly over 3 percent in future years. Corporate profits despite lags have historically held inflation, which is likely to run at 3–5 percent. Our selectivity remains at 9 percent, but even if it fell to 3–6 percent, this could result in a total estimated appreciation of over 15 percent a year."

"This analysis leads us to the conclusion that it is possible to make discriminatory judgments from our market universe and, although we have seen a most unusual market, we are presented with the time in which our approach should be most valuable. The principal question then becomes not so much what has happened, but do we own the correct securities for the next phase? . . .

"The market decline in the past quarter, painful as it has been, has given us an opportunity to increase the expected total return of your portfolio at prices in relation to value unseen for two decades. That we have been able to do so and increase the income yield seems all the more unusual. Our program during the quarter has not been a radical change but has involved the sale of some securities that were cheap to buy others that were even cheaper and had better historical growth rates."

Date: October 1974   Culmination of Two-Year
                                      Sharp Bear Market

". . . There are two paramount questions. First, will the market decline further? Second, does the extent of the decline presage a depression as it did forty-five years ago?

"Two years ago, we expressed the view that 102 on the S&P 500 was very high and we expected our selectivity skill and lower volatility than most investors would give our accounts comparative resistivity—if required. This relative resistivity was accomplished. But the extent of the decline was unexpected, influenced as it was by a number of events that were entirely unforeseen by us and most others: 12 percent interest rates, 10 percent inflation, oil crises, stalled government, and international financial strains. A few things are happening as expected: a mild recession, an increase in investor appreciation of yield, a correction of speculative excesses in normally investment-grade securities, and a continuation of Batterymarch selection skills of several percentage points a year against a random selection of all stocks. We have gone on a journey we wish we had avoided but, having done so, we are reluctant to leave the wagon that has always before made the return trip.

"Market technicians, who I believe have a good sense of market history, tell me that the normal three downward waves of a decline conform to anticipation of problems, appraisal of current problems, and the most unpredictable phase—an emotional liquidation that seemingly defies quantification. If this breakdown provides a guide to where we are, we passed through the reasonable-value stage earlier in the year. Prices now are dictated by the forced liquidation of individuals and institutions saying that no further declines can be withstood, even if the odds would favor a reversal. Furthermore, investment managers may be frozen into inactivity by threats of job security and a pattern of ego-shattering decisions in the past couple of years. The combination of noneconomic-induced selling and hesitant potential buyers produced a third stage decline of determinable character but indeterminant extent and duration. To the extent that this last phase has plunged prices well below those hoped for by the classical value-oriented investor, unusual once-in-a-generation opportunities exist. After all, we have already paid for once-in-a-generation risks.

"Most institutions have acquired at least double their normal cash positions. If a 10 percent cash position was held two years ago and the equity account declines by 50 percent or so, the cash is now 20 percent without making any assertive sales. In many institutional accounts, there is some cash flow, which by manager preference or client dictate, will not be employed until 'conditions seem more secure'. The nearly unanimous consensus view is that these cash positions can be reduced promptly whenever investors all see the same secure signs. Estimates on the size of temporarily sidelined cash vary but the magnitude is easily in the tens of billions.

"In dealing with the central issue—to invest in equities or not, and if yes, how much—we can summarize our views as:

1. We don't know when or where the decline will end, but it seems to be overdue and overdone by most historical and fundamental standards.

2. More so than at anytime in Batterymarch's history, our portfolios seem to have exceptional investment potential.

3. Institutional cash levels are being determined more by psychological conditions than economic necessity. These levels can be subject to extreme change."

We send detailed, quantitative reports to our clients that stress almost any aspect one wishes to study. Portfolio values are unitized like a mutual fund so that they can be compared in performance with standard market indices with income added in, as well as with published mutual-fund figures and most of the figures used by other investment managers.

Percentage results of gross account values are so misleading as to be useless for performance determination because there always is some cash flow in or out. Since most investment managers are oriented to tax-free accounts, total return or the sum of appreciation and income without adjustment for taxes is the appropriate measure.

In addition to the detailed performance track, accounts are presented in the conventional balance-sheet way, with a breakdown by type of asset, industry, estimated income, and the like. Some investment managers, like ourselves, highlight the differences between cost and market, showing in clear form unrealized gains and losses. There is no doubt that such procedure accentuates the impression of good results under bull-market conditions and poor results in a bear market.

This illumination further accentuates the likelihood that investment managers will eliminate their losses so that they fade out of sight, rather than become continually festering sores in the client-manager relationship. An investment manager can make a loss disappear, although overall performance will continue to be penalized by the amount of loss that is taken.

The face-to-face meetings with investment commit-
tees of institutional clients are especially intriguing. It is frequently an adversary proceeding when the client feels he
must pick up the flaws that are present in every portfolio.
From the manager's standpoint, it is a salesmanship activity
to renew a client's confidence in the fact that the high objectives that were originally established are likely to be met if
only patience will be exercised.

Some of the most interesting meetings with clients
take place in the first days of a new management activity.
Shortly after Batterymarch was selected to manage the endowment for a private school, the regular quarterly meeting
of its investment committee was held at the University Club
in New York. The account was split three ways: part to the
Common Fund, the newly established co-mingled fund for
small educational institutions; part with T. Rowe Price,
with its emphasis on institutionally acceptable growth
stocks; and part with Batterymarch for our low-multiple,
high-yield, value orientation.

The finance committee had two sections. One consisted of ladies who were graduates of the school, largely the
benefactresses in the alumnae-giving program. They were influential in setting the tone for the trustees but were not
especially familiar with the investment process. The second
section included men who were engaged in some aspect of
the investment business. One was managing partner of a
brokerage firm, another was president of a large mutual
fund, and so on.

Batterymarch had converted a cash portfolio into one
with a 60 percent securities position, most of which were un-
known names in relatively mundane industries. In our opinion, the securities offered the best combination of value at
low risk.

One of the influential members of the committee was

an elderly Wall Street lawyer. From the end of the table he watched me enter the room and lowered his head to see my face over his half-glasses. His eyes narrowed, and as I sat down to arrange my papers, he said, " Mr. LeBaron, I hope you will tell me this morning about these speculations (stabbing the portfolio in front of him with a forefinger) you have purchased for our girls."

Considering that this was the first time I had met this committee and new relationships are always initially unsettling, I reached for a coffee cup on a side table to add some liquid to my parched throat. With more than the normal rustle of papers, I began my comments. "Gentlemen"—then looking around the room—"and Ladies. Before I begin with our outlook for the market and the economy, let me tell you that I will depart from my usual format. Let us, instead, just take every security we have put in the portfolio, as well as others we propose to add in the next several months, and discuss one by one the features which appeal to us."

I then proceeded to list each security and say approximately the same thing, because each one more or less matched our profile of selling below book value, at double the yield of the market, at half the market multiple, and at twice the rate of growth of the average security. I discussed the businesses that each was engaged in: one controlled barge traffic, another was a water utility, still another was in building maintenance, and so on.

We dissected each one, taking more than an hour for this exercise. There were no questions; in fact, no indications that anyone was even listening. At the end of the session, the initial questioner looked up and said; "Mr. Le-Baron, I haven't seen such values since the early thirties. I didn't know that it was possible in this raging, speculative bull market the youngsters have produced to find things like this."

Many other client sessions are not so heartening. In some, the investment manager has a feeling that nothing he does is right. In the light of our 20x20 hindsight vision, all of us have impressions that if we had done something different, it would have produced better results. These committee sessions tend to have a large measure of hindsight on the part of the committee members and rationalization on the part of the investment manager.

It is my impression that when confidence deteriorates between client and investment manager, it rarely returns and the relationship might just as well be terminated. Capricious switching of investment advisors is not only nonproductive, but may be counterproductive. It is very expensive for the investment manager to produce the extra effort required to become familiar with a new client. From the client's standpoint, one portfolio is invariably sold and replaced by another with high commission and transaction costs.

Face-to-face communication seems expensive and at the time not especially productive. It is essential, however, so long as the investment manager feels he is providing both results and confidence. There seems no other way to achieve it.

Some client meetings are in a stricter format, usually a presentation to a group of six to ten. The following is an abbreviated version of one made to a corporate client in August 1974:

"The Vietnam War has just ended. The nightmare referred to in President Ford's talk was thought by many to be Watergate, but it was Viet Nam. After fifteen years of inflation, abuse of power, and deterioration of U.S. stature in the world, we have reached a conclusion to this terrible period. The dispiritedness and demoralization of the American people should soon absolve.

"In this talk I will cover three things: first, the macro-issues, which at this juncture are going to be most important in determining the performance of the account. This will form a background for our investment strategy. It essentially describes the external environment in which you work in your business and we work in the investment field.

"Second, I will describe briefly our own investment philosophy. We are somewhat unique in our approach and much of what we do only makes sense if you can see it through our eyes. Our investment philosophy is, by contrast to the macroissues, more the internal workings of the firm and recognition of the market mechanism. Much of the external environment in prices is discounted already at today's market levels.

"We may differ from others, but I applaud the approach of those who pursue similar specialized, though different, tacks. We emphasize low risk, but that is due more to the stress we see being placed by others in high-risk areas rather than to provincial Boston conservatism.

"Finally, let's see how we've applied our general posture to your account.

"In terms of macroissues, I think the times look very similar to the early twenties. There is a great degree of financial strain, as there was then. Business is likely to slow down modestly in terms of real growth because we've had an enormous bulge in the satisfaction of consumer demands. And there is a general desire for peace and quiet in this country.

"One of the very strong pluses this time, which may make the period we are entering different from the twenties, is that the Third World now has the wherewithal to satisfy its needs through higher raw-material prices. I'm sure many of you remember Barbara Ward's *Rich Nations, Poor Nations,* which describes the ever-widening gap in wealth between rich and poor nations. That gap should now close, which would resolve a potentially unresolvable source of conflict.

"Inflation is in the forefront of all our minds. I expect it will remain in the 10 percent area and we'll get used to it, just as it stayed in the 5 percent area after being at 2 percent. We became accustomed to that also. I don't believe that inflation is negative for the stock market. It may be a neutral or a plus to the extent that equities are a call on real assets. But inflation does complicate business decision-making and it introduces a new element of uncertainty in business and investment thinking.

"In terms of a recession, I conclude that we entered a European-type recession in November 1973. Whether we started it because it was induced by tight money, or tight oil, makes little difference. King Faisal and Arthur Burns were in partnership. We'll emerge from it sometime this year; perhaps we're coming out now.

"This will be the first recession in this country with higher profits, although that has been the pattern in Europe with its steeper inflationary trend. The long-term trend that we keep in mind is that the United States is becoming increasingly like Europe. Certainly so in currency where the dollar is now just one of a number of world currencies. Social attitudes are being Europeanized with emphasis on more unionization, on holidays, work rules, and the like.

"In politics we probably will enter a period of legislative-dominated government, slower real growth—likely to be on a 1½ to 3 percent pattern rather than a 3 to 4 percent pattern—with emphasis on quality of life in the West and standard of living in the Third World. Inflation rates should range between 5 and 10 percent with more clustering near the higher than the lower end of that range. Finally, I think the stock market will do much better in the next five years than it has done in the last. I see no reason to change the same forecast I made five years ago for an inverse relationship.

"Our own investment philosophy relates to market efficiency and market capitalization. We emphasize stock selection in the size category just smaller than that which is dominated by institutional investors. We concentrate on individually owned securities that are institutionally acceptable.

"We consider that institutions are great experts at pricing securities, but that individuals are less well informed and have less acute judgment. We are searching continually for unexploited values, stocks that seem perhaps 30 percent undervalued compared with others in their own universe. We imagine we are buying the entire company. If the price rises to normal value, the security becomes the candidate for a sale. Now it may have a random chance of going up or down.

"We operate this way principally for low risk; secondarily, as a way to make money. The opportunities for money making in this activity are greater now than at any time we have seen over the past five years. This is because of the enormous disenchantment with what is called the second tier. We are very price conscious and we look at things like discretionary cash flow instead of just earnings per share, which may be the accountant's guess of what future cash flows will be like. Companies that fit both the economic framework and our own philosophy are the ones that will find their way into the portfolios we manage.

"Let's deal with your portfolio specifically. We have been operating for two months and are now 70 percent of the way toward a complete transition of a Batterymarch portfolio. That is on target, as we generally like to take something on the order of a quarter to complete the transition. Normally, we would have moved a little faster, but in this type of sloppy market, the markets have been thin and prices have been deceptive. There has not been as much depth to the prices as we like. We expect the portfolio to be equity-oriented, as the expected total returns are much higher in equities than in bonds. A 9 percent bond and a 10 percent inflation rate sound to me like a backward step.

"The portfolio is balanced—50 percent cyclical and 50 percent defensive. This is slightly more in a cyclical direction than our composite portfolio, but at this stage of the recession, looking to the future, we are building up the cyclical aspect of other accounts to match the posture we have in your account. Three months from now, or by the end of 1974, I expect to be 60 to 70 percent cyclical, with the remainder defensive.

"Within the defensive area, banks and insurance, traditionally a strong area for us, are 15 percent. We would normally be larger than this, but there are a number of imponderables about the financial condition of banks and insurance companies that we are attempting to grapple with. But market prices, in my view, should more than compensate for the imponderables. In the next month to six weeks, I expect the bank and insurance position to move up into the 20 percent area. Cash in 7 percent, which is slightly lower than our target at this juncture of 10 percent. The target yield is 6.3 percent, or almost double that for the market as a whole. If we take a return on cash as well, we come up to better than 6–1/2 percent.

"The portfolio is priced at 5.5 times latest twelve months' earnings, or something less than the average stock, which is about 7 times latest twelve months' earnings, or about half as much as the S&P 500. The rate of growth for the past ten years is about 10 percent for the portfolio as a whole, or about double that for the entire economy.

"We expect this portfolio will be slightly less volatile than the S&P 500 in down and up markets with better results than the market average obtained by 3 to 5 percent selectivity. We are operating in a universe that is not crowded by other institutional investors. Finally, our focus is on 1976 in portfolio construction. Every bit of work we've done suggests that the next six to twelve months is in the price, even in our area. The investment manager who can project his mind beyond that area is likely to do the best job for his clients."

8

Ideology of
Security Markets -
A Forecast

We began with the proposition that security markets are efficient and gave a number of illustrations and episodes on why that is a valid hypothesis. A study of the blending of education, motivation, and communication within the market structures leads to the energy-tapping, self-canceling, isometric-exercise equilibrium of an institutionally dominated market. These observations should be enough to help understand the real workings of the system as it is and not as the self-serving statements of the industry so often portrayed. Yet, as a practicing financial analyst, I cannot resist the occupational responsibility to make a forecast or two.

Return to Sobriety

The last several decades in the investment business have been fun. To be sure the most recent bear market has left a number of professionals on the unemployment lines and they are not smiling. For the most part they had a wealth of experiences in the "good old days" in which their brilliance was recognized and they successfully displayed heroics by making a lot of money, cultivating interesting people, and imagining what it would be like to retire at forty. It was fun for client and agent. Even the government man enjoyed going after the big fraud: the young wheeler-dealer who puts a conglomerate together to snare the naive and the hopeful. The academic enjoyed his self-righteousness in unfrocking the investment specialist with naked computer studies proclaiming "random walk" and challenging the industry to the accountability of cost-effectiveness. Those days have gone.

Work in the investment field is going to be demanding, workaday drudgery. There will be a few places for creative people, but the rest of the business will be staffed by operators. It is going to be like an insurance company: serious, responsible business.

Structural Humpty-Dumpty

The king's men will not be able to put all the old pieces together again. Instead some new characters will get up on the wall. It is worth listening, for an exercise in antilogic, to a securities-brokerage leader commenting publicly upon his return from the Virgin Islands where he attended a meeting of the industry to discuss poor profit margins.

The traditional roles of selling by a broker, responding by an institution, and soliciting by a company are no longer appropriate. To talk about what they used to do is not addressing the future but the broken past. No one, NO ONE, of stature in the investment industry points out future needs and new structural requirements. They don't even admit how the business operates now.

The old pieces are broken and will be left shattered. New entities for swift, inexpensive executions will emerge. Recorded phone messages from company financial officials will replace the expensive company investment visit by jet. Reliance upon quantitative data will place new demands upon accountants for numbers that have some relevance to the investment decision rather than merely satisfying some old adherence to a cost-accounting text.

Costs Will Be Reduced

It is clear that investors are willing to share part of their security profits with the operators of the system. It is similarly clear that they are unwilling to part with their capital base for a job poorly done. If the system is unfair or too expensive, they exercise their option by withdrawing voluntarily. Expenses in the securities industry are estimated at $7 billion including underwriting, commissions, management fees, custody charges, and so on. On a total capital base that may be about one trillion, this figure is an annual seven-tenths of 1 percent toll. If the average annual return on capital is 12 percent, the administrative costs are 6 percent of the annual return—much too high if we are going to work harder at demanding a higher return on scarce capital. A reduction in the proportion of return allocated to the securities industry costs means loss of jobs and firms. There is no way one can reduce $7 billion without lifting badge numbers.

What is a fair number? As a guess, no more than 1 or 2 percent of the annual capital return could be used in support of the capital-allocation system. That estimate implies a reduction of 60 to 80 percent of gross revenues for the securities industry. Yes, the stock and bond markets as we know them today will be dead, but that does not mean that their replacements may not flourish.

Expanded Regulation

Self-regulation in the securities field has failed. Government will take a greater role in the regulatory process and even sponsor change if the industry does not. Specifically, the concept of full disclosure has serious inequities. The interpretation of what is being disclosed varies according to the sophistication of the analyst. Investment practice will be scrutinized by a government agency to see if it is grounded in documentable precedent, a testing procedure not unlike what the Food & Drug Administration requires for new drugs.

Functional Interchangeability

Responsibility for the future course of the investment field rests on the proper balance of government, academia, and institutions. Until now they have been separate, self-serving entities each propounding its special interest. There has just begun to be an exchange in roles through consulting relationships. These will grow to regular job exchanges along the European system of interrelation among business, government, and university. Efficiency will be one result at the expense of competitiveness.

1985

The year is 1985. There is a Federal Stock Exchange located in Washington that is completely electronic, processing capital transfers as electronic pulses at a cost of 1¢ a transfer. The specialist book is on a CRT with instant execution and instant funds transferred by machine. Trading volume is hundreds of times greater than today's and markets are broad and liquid. The government is a trader in equities for its own account (isn't it already a ½ owner with corporate taxes and regulation); investors will place orders each morning by machine ("here is what I want my account to look like"); machines will return a calculation on the cost and probability of getting there and the investor will say yea or nay and it is done. Company names in a portfolio will mean no more than division names do now to an investor. They are a means to a portfolio and not the end itself. Clients will monitor the details of a manager's activity on a daily, real time basis, or hire an inspector to do it for them. All investment activities will be "in the clear" and closely regulated. Money raising for companies will be easy, cheap and instantaneous *at the marginal price*. Companies can buy and sell their own securities without a special registration with their intentions to purchase an "open hand" like everyone else. This end may justify the pain of transition and the anxiety of uncertainty a decade ago.

I have ended where I began in 1960 . . . by giving a memo on the future of the investment business. Here my boss is not one managing partner of a brokerage firm but investors and investment colleagues whose esteem I cherish. In the earlier case my document was returned with the admonition that my only task was to sell. I wonder if the environment has really changed in fifteen years or will the same thing happen again? Perhaps in that response I will have my basis for a forecast.

Index